Decolonizing the Foundations of American Indian Law

Victoria Sutton, MPA, PhD, JD

American Indian Legal History Series

VARGAS PUBLISHING

ISBN-978-0-9968186-8-1

Manufactured in the United States of America
First printing, 2021

Cover design and illustration by Victoria Sutton

Published and distributed by
Vargas Publishing
P.O. Box 6801
Lubbock, TX   79466
http://vargaspublishing.com

Table of Contents

Dedicated to

my American Indian ancestors

Elizabeth Culom

and

She-la Bird

Introduction

This book explores the foundations of American Indian Law and specifically, federal Indian Law from both the colonizer's view but with perspectives from a Native American Indian individual and tribal nation viewpoint. Decolonizing here means to consider the unequal power distribution and the coded language used with objectives of racial and governmental domination or subjugation of tribes and their people. This deconstruction of U.S. Supreme Court opinions is necessary to form a way forward. Finding a pathway through precedent to reverse destructive colonizing language, principles and actions that started in the foundations of American Indian Law is critical to moving forward.

Your first thoughts upon an initial readings of American Indian Law may have been that surely these cases are no longer relevant or no longer law given their racial biases and often overt unfairness? But they are. They also bring with them the colonizers views that can be appallingly ignorant and shockingly racist. Your next thought might be, then why do we not just unravel all of these cases and invalidate their holdings and start over? That might be technically possible, but it would undo commitments, policies, treaties and law that tribes as well as anyone interacting with tribes have come to rely on in investing time, resources and their future. To invalidate all of American Indian Law could lead to the biggest constitutional Fifth Amendment takings cases in our history, requiring the U.S. to compensate tribes and non-tribal individuals who had relied upon these cases for investments. But more importantly for the colonizer, it would invalidate all the land transactions that put the title of aboriginal and Indian lands into the hands of the conquers.

Questions like: Who is an Indian? What is an Indian tribe? How can tribes have sovereignty, yet be dominated by

1

the laws and actions of the United States are questions we explore in this book.

The book begins with the historical development of federal Indian law and provide the opinions of the court in some landmark cases, important to Indian law today. Perspectives of tribes and some of the background for these cases is provided which is often complex and history not covered in traditional courses.

Legal history of the indigenous peoples of the United States influences every new problem in Indian Country that arises for resolution before a court of law, today. Legal precedents from before the ratification of the United States Constitution, are also often binding and controlling in many issues.

American Indian law is generally considered to be shaped not only by legal principles but according to the Indian Policy at the time period. The Indian Policy periods are typically divided into nine periods in United States history: Colonial (1492-1776); Confederation (1776-1778); Trade and Intercourse (1789-1835); Removal (1835-1861); Reservation (1861-1887); Allotment and Assimilation (1871-1934); Indian Reorganization Act (1934-1940); Termination (1940-1962); and Self-Determination (1962 - present). The governmental actions taken by the Executive Branch, Congress and the Judicial Branch, can be best understood by considering the policy period in which the action was taken.

Historical Periods of Indian Law and Policy – the Colonizer View

Colonial Period (1492-1776)

France, Britain and Spain were the primary colonizers of the New World, although Portugal and Switzerland attempted to make a foothold in the New World as early as in the late 1500s to the early 1700s. Each of these Nations differed in their approaches to indigenous peoples. France typically approached the interaction by assimilating with the Indians; Britain was primarily interested in trade and commerce; while Spain was more interested in enslaving Indians for their labor.

During the colonial period, the foundations of the legal relationship between the new country and the indigenous people of America was an important issue facing those who hoped to settle in the New World. European theorists asked questions about the morality and legality of possessing land discovered in America. Two leading theorists were Dominican clerics Bartolome de las Casas (1474-1566) and Francisco de Vitoria (1486-1547). De las Casas had been a missionary among the Indians and was able to discuss the abuses of Spanish colonization, from his own first hand experiences. He criticized the Spanish *encomienda* system which granted the Spanish land and the right to enslave Indians to do their work. Vitoria, on the other hand, had never been to the New World, however he did agree with De las Casas on the humanity of the indigenous peoples.

Vitoria set forth the legal relationship that would be the foundation of American Indian law. He held that Indians possessed an entitlement to the land and the right to act autonomously, and this, the Europeans must respect. This evidenced the influence of theology on his concept of law, with God as the source of legal authority. Vitoria supported the idea that Indians were rational human beings. This was in conflict with what many believed was the bestowal of ownership to Spain over all the lands discovered, not ruled by Christians, as granted by Pope Alexander VI. Therefore, it was important to find that Indians were human and rational in order to convert them to Christianity, which was a job expected of Spain by the Catholic Church.

But how did Vitoria reason that Spain could ultimately claim the lands? First, Vitoria concluded that the Indians were not suited for the administration of government which brought civility and control over life. If Spain could provide this government — for their benefit of course — then this would in effect allow Spain to control the land. This laid the foundation for the understanding of the trust relationship between the federal government and Indians in modern American Indian law. Second, Vitoria reasoned that under a natural law theory, that Indians had obligations as well as rights, which allowed visitors, travelers, traders and churches on their missions to convert. Should the indigenous peoples resist this obligation, then the Spanish would be morally justified, under a just war theory, to fight and conquer the Indians. Thus, the foundation for the conquer's right to possession of the land. Because of the rights held by Indians, the use of treaties was seen as a way to gain the consent of the indigenous peoples with the domination of the colonizers.

[from S. James Anaya, Indigenous Peoples in International Law 2d ed. Oxford Press 2004].

The failure of Spain to heed the advice of Vitoria, in respecting the land and rights of the indigenous people led to the Pueblo Revolt of 1620. A landmark event for the Pueblo people, the harsh rule of the Spanish and Mexicans was turned back after more than one hundred years of colonization aggression. This event is a pivotal landmark in Pueblo government and history, today, and the events which surrounded the Pueblo Revolt of 1620 are important even in today's governance among the Pueblo people in the

Southwestern United States.

There are many treaties with tribes with nations that did not win the colonizing war. Treaties with tribes on the East Coast of the U.S. were made with Switzerland (you have heard of New Bern, North Carolina?). There are treaties between tribes and Spain in those historically colonized areas of Florida, Texas and California (the Treaty of Guadalupe Hidalgo, for example).

One of the early treaties, The Treaty of Middle Plantation 1677, was made between the Indians of Virginia and the Colony of Virginia. Upon Virginia entering the United States, the treaties and agreements made by the colony were assumed by the new Commonwealth of Virginia.

The Treaty of Middle Plantation began with a recognition of the sovereignty of King Charles II, by the paying of tribute by the Indians to the King. This paying of tribute has been a continuous practice for more than three hundred years, based on the Treaty of Middle Plantation, when all of the Virginia tribes come to pay tribute to the Governor of Virginia, bringing venison (deer meat), fish or turkeys.

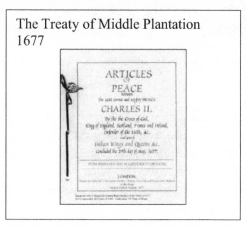

The Treaty of Middle Plantation 1677

Wife of Gov. Davis accepts the tribute in 1919.

Pamunkey Chief, Tecumseh D. Cook, delivering tribute to Gov. Allmond in 1959.

Virginia tribes paying tribute to Gov. McAuliffe (2012).
Evanne Armour/Nexstar Capitol Bureau

The second and third articles, reproduced below, set forth the way in which the Indians would hold their land, agreeing never to disturb their ownership, as long as they remained loyal to the English. The twenty-two articles of the Treaty, set forth other agreements that Indians would continue to govern within their existing tribal nations, that they can travel and hunt (as long as they obtain a permit), relations with other tribes, translators, and negotiating differences rather than going to war.

II. That thereupon the said Indian Kings &
Queens and their Subjects shall hold their lands,
and have the same confirmed to them and their
posterity by Patent under the Seale of this his
Magesties Colony, without any fee gratuity or
Reward for ye same, in such sort, and in as free
and firme manner as others his Magesties Liege
Subjects, have and enjoye their Lands, and
possessions, paying onely yearly for, and in Liew of
a Quitrent or acknowledgement for the same three
Indian Arrowes.
III. That all Indians who are in amity with us, &
have not land siffitient to plant up, be upon
information forthwith provided for, and land laid
out, and confirmed to them as affores'd never to be
disturbed therein, or taken from them, soe long as
they owne keep and maintaine the due obedience
& Subjection to his Majestie his Govern'r and
Government; & amity & friendship towards the
English.

The policy of colonization, typified by this Treaty
expresses more humility by the colonizers as they seek the
good favor of the tribal Nations to assist them in their
colonizing efforts. Article IV of the Treaty gives us a sense of
apology from the English for causing the Indians to retaliate
for wrongs done to them by the English:

IV. Whereas by the mutuall discontents,
Complaints, jealousies, and feares of English and
Indians occasioned by the violent intrusions of
divers English into their lands, forceing the Indians
by way of Revenge, to kill the Cattle & hoggs of

7

the English, whereby offence, and injuries being
given, and done on boeth sides, the peace of this his
Majesties Colony hath bin much disturbed, and the
late unhappy Rebellion by this means in a great
measure begunne & fomented which hath involved
this Country into soe much Ruine, & misery, for
prevention of which injuries and evill consequences
as much as possible we may for time to come it is
hereby concluded and enacted that noe English,
shall seate or plant nearer then three miles of any
Indian towne . . .

A period of treatymaking brought hundreds of agreements along the eastern seaboard between tribes and colonies that were needed for their efforts at colonization and prioritizing trade:

1679 - Albany Conference (permitted Iroquois to hunt and travel trough Manahoac lands, blocked Algonquian tribes in Tidewater from Piedmont)

1684 - Albany treaty signed by Lord Howard (blocked English settlement in Iroquois-controlled Piedmont, restricting Northern Virginia occupation to Tidewater area)

1722 - Treaty of Albany (restricted Iroquois to west of the Blue Ridge)

1744 - Treaty of Lancaster (Iroquois sold Virginia their claims of lands "to the setting sun," pushing them out of Shenandoah Valley to west of the Alleghenies)

1748 - Virginia and Pennsylvania distribute gifts to Ohio River tribes at Logstown (part of competition with French traders)

1752 - Treaty of Logstown (limited Delaware and Shawnee claims south of the Ohio River)

1768 - Treaties of Fort Stanwix and Hard Labor

1770 - Treaty of Lochaber (ceding title to the lands north of the Ohio River to the English)

1775 - Treaty of Sycamore Shoals (limited Cherokee claims in far Southwestern Virginia)

1777 - Treaty of Long Island (limited Cherokee claims in far Southwestern Virginia)

The next major treaty was the Treaty of Hopewell with the Cherokees, November 28th, 1785, 7 Stat. 18, which established the frontier boundary and opened a floodgate of new settlement in Virginia and North Carolina.

During this period, the Trade Wars were brought on by the lack of a cohesive national policy of promoting free trade between the colonies and the tribes, due to the proprietary nature of the colonies. The Trade Wars in Virginia and the Carolinas were fiercely carried on, at the highest levels of their governments. In 1698, the South Carolina House of Commons proposed legislation to forbid Virginia traders to trade with any South Carolina Indian. That bill failed along with a 1701 legislative proposal that goods of all Virginia traders be confiscated when in South Carolina. However, a bill to tax horses being brought from Virginia into South Carolina did pass. The stated purpose was "Care be taken to bring the Catawba Indians more dependent on this Goverment: by discourageing the Virginia tradeing among them."

Virginians, however despite the law, continued to trade with the Indians of South Carolina, and on June 13, 1707, the South Carolina Commons House recommended to the Governor that he seize the Virginia Indian traders, "if it may be done by the Laws of England." The House was not sure if this was legal, but determined that a 1703 Act which required an export duty of three pence on every deerskin and beaver skin taken out of the colony provided for arrest of violators. So in 1707, the Carolina government invoked the law and confiscated the pelts of a Virginia trader who had left his pelts in a Catawba town for safekeeping.

The Virginia trader immediately petitioned the Commons House for redress, but was told it was not in their jurisdiction to decide. Later, the Board of Trade and Plantations wrote a letter to the lord proprietors of the South Carolina colony asking whether the seizure was "done by virtue of any orders from Your Lordships and upon what grounds . . ."

A year later, the Lord Proprietors responded in a letter that the seizure was for the failure of the Virginians to pay the export levies on the pelts, but that there was no law to forbid their trading in South Carolina. The Virginia traders then went to the Colonial Council in Williamsburg which was the seat of power in the colonies, April 28, 1708. The traders were able to get some of their goods returned, but were prohibited from crossing into South Carolina in the future. The open trade wars began.

The Virginia Colonial Council wrote the Governor of South Carolina saying that:

> . . . this manner of proceeding is althogether new and unprecedented that her Majesty first by her royall instructions granted and afterwards confirmed by Law a free trade to all the inhabitants of this Coilony with all Indians watsoever . . . therefore the Government of South Carolina hav no authority to monopolize all the Indian trade.

The Virginia Council then issued passports to its

traders.

The matter was taken to Queen Anne, who responded on September 26, 1709, but her letter did not arrive until April 1710, and said that she decreed that the Virginians be permitted to trade freely with the "Western Indians" without interference from South Carolina." South Carolina continued to place burdens on the traders, and began requiring that they travel to Charleston to get permits to trade with the Indians — a trip of at least a couple hundred miles out of the way of the trading path. Finally, even those Virginians who obtained permits were questioned and their goods were confiscated. Queen Anne and the Privy Council acted in January 1713, to disallow the action taken by the South Carolinians, taking another year to arrive in the colonies. [Excerpted from Douglas Summers Brown, *The Catawba Indians, The People of the River*, 110-114 (1966)]

Native Americans were essential to the success of these propriety colonies and so honoring treaties and encouraging peace was a priority for the colonists. Religion also continued to be important with Christianization of Indians continuing as a mission for the colonists, in some ways, justifying their taking their land.

Confederation (1776-1788)

During this period of time, the Articles of Confederation were written, which addressed the important trade issues with Indians and Indian tribal nations. The Indian nations were in a strong political position with the United States, which had just declared its independence from Great Britain. Alliances with other Nations on the part of Indian tribes led to the need to use treaties to gain trust and certainty with the Indian Nations.

This was also a time when states and individuals were making deals with tribal nations as well as individual Native Americans to acquire land, resulting in a great deal of confusion and conflict over land title and tribal control over their own collective tribal lands. Despite the fact that individuals could not sell their own tribe's land, several unfortunate incidents led to vast losses of land due to unauthorized individuals selling land that belonged to the tribe.

Trade and Intercourse Period (1789-1835)

It was the trade wars among the colonies, like those described above, which led to the discussion at the Constitutional Convention that a mere amendment to the Articles of Confederation would not cure these trade war problems. Influenced primarily by the trade with the Indians and the trade wars, the Constitutional Convention determined that a commerce clause must be written in a new Constitution, because this omission made the Articles of Confederation unworkable. This led to what is called the Indian Commerce Clause, and is one of the three mentions of Indians as a race, in the United States Constitution.

The U.S. Constitution was written and ratified in 1789, and the importance of the relationship with Indians and Indian Nations is evident. Indians are the only race specifically mentioned in the U.S. Constitution, and they are mentioned three times. The Indian Commerce Clause states that the federal government will have control over trade and commerce with the Indians.

This critical time laid the foundation for land ownership and trade issues with the Indians and Indian Nations. The Trade and Intercourse Act was passed in 1789 and 1791 (25 U.S.C. §177), gave control over land purchases from Indians and trade with the Indians to the new federal government, and prohibited individuals and states from buying land from Indians. Prior to this, individuals may have been prohibited from buying land from Indians by their state laws, but states were continuing to buy land from Indians. The reason for the control over trade was because the states had created a series of "trade wars" between themselves in order to keep commerce within their borders, essentially stopping the free flow of commerce which would be essential to the building of a new nation.

Thomas Jefferson reflected on the rights of American Indians to their property when he confessed that natural rights were not applied to the actions of the Europeans in taking lands from American Indians:

> *[W]hoever shall attempt to trace the claims of the European nations to the countrys [sic] in America from the principles of Justice, or reconcile the invasions made on the Native Indians to the natural rights of mankind, will find that he is pursuing a Chimera, which exists only in his own imagination, against the evidence of indisputable facts.*

[Wilcomb E. Washburn, *The Moral and Legal Justifications for Dispossessing the Indians, in* Seventeenth Century America: Essays on Colonial History 15, 26 (James M. Smith ed., 1959)].

The United States Supreme Court, the third branch of the new federal government, was established with its first Chief Justice John Jay. But it was not until the second Chief Justice, John Marshall, was appointed, did the Court address the legal relationship between Indian nations and the United States.

Justice John Marshall was born in western Virginia on the frontier, and it is certain he had encounters with the Cherokees and many other tribes that traveled down the Appalachian Mountain ridges. He served in Gen. Washington's Army, and was part of the notorious battle where Gen. Lee retreated against the orders of Gen. Washington. He rose in the ranks to become an Associate Judge Advocate of the U.S. Army, and participated in the trial of Benedict Arnold. He was also distantly related to Thomas

Jefferson, also of Virginia. He was steeped in the visceral role of founding the United States, and now he was critical to interpreting the key document that would direct the moral and legal direction of the new nation. How he interpreted the sordid history of the colonists relationship with the tribal nations in the context of their status in the U.S. Constitution would form the foundation cases that influence all of federal Indian Law. [Albert J. Beveridge, *The Life of John Marshall in four volumes* (1916)].

Tribal nations were specifically named as a third sovereignty in the U.S. Constitution in the Commerce Clause, and that would ensure the continuity of their own self-determination but not for the reasons of morality and fairness one might imagine. The first judicial opinion had a lot more to do with the new government having good title to the massive land acquisitions from the tribes, and less to do with "fairness" to tribes and Native Americans. The second opinions, known as the Cherokee cases, were about building a judicially cognizable justification for taking tribal and aboriginal land in exchange for allowing the continued existence and self-governance of tribes as sovereign bodies. Defining what that sovereignty meant within the boundaries of another sovereign nation was the task of Justice Marshall

The Federal Indian Law Trilogy

The federal Indian law foundation cases — referred to as the Marshall trilogy, establish the legal relationship between tribes and the United States in the context of the U.S. Constitution. These cases were written by Chief Justice John Marshall, who, in these three cases, defined the way federal Indian law cases are decided today. These three cases attempted to resolve land and self-government issues.

The first of these judicial decisions that provided the foundation for all subsequent federal Indian law in the United States was decided by the U.S. Supreme Court in 1823 in a case called **Johnson v. McIntosh**.[1] This opinion established that land grants made by tribal chiefs to individuals from 1773 to 1775 — prior to the establishment of the United States— were valid. Basing this decision on the "right of occupancy", at the sufferance of the United States, the court held that Indians *did* have rights to convey. (To find otherwise, would have been to invalidate treaties which gave immense tracts of land to the colonial and U.S. governments.) The court further established that the "doctrine of discovery" and "title by conquer," had evolved into the current system of controlling land of the tribes which had been conquered. Chief Justice John Marshall wrote in *Johnson v. McIntosh*, 21 U.S. (8 Wheat.) 543 (1823), that whatever the "original justice of the claim," and however "opposed to natural right, and to the usages of civilized nations," he was constrained in doing justice for Indian peoples because he sat in the "Courts of the conqueror." Establishing title in the sovereign was possible with some restraints, "when the conquest is complete, and the conquered inhabitants can be blended with the conquerors, or safely governed as a distinct people."[2]

Further, Justice Marshall found that taking land was a considered a righteous bargain because the Indians received

---

[1] Johnson v. McIntosh, 21 U.S. (8 Wheat.) 543 (1823).
[2] Johnson v. McIntosh, 21 U.S. (8 Wheat.) 543 (1823).

Christianity and unlimited independent for their land. He wrote:

> *The potentates of the old world found no difficulty in convincing themselves that they made ample compensation to the inhabitants of the new by bestowing on them civilization and Christianity in exchange for unlimited independence.* [*Johnson v. McIntosh*, 21 U.S. (8 Wheat.) 543, 573 (1823)]

The following excerpt of that case, explains the court's reasoning as to how the United States could hold a valid title to the land in the United States.

Johnson and Graham's Lessee v. M'Intosh
Supreme Court of the United States
21 U.S. 543 (Feb 28, 1823)

Conquest gives a title which the Courts of the conqueror cannot deny, whatever the private and speculative opinions of individuals may be, respecting the original justice of the claim which has been successfully asserted. The British government, which was then our government, and whose rights have passed to the United States, asserted a title to all the lands occupied by Indians, within the chartered limits of the British colonies. It asserted also a limited sovereignty over them, and the exclusive right of extinguishing the title which occupancy gave to them. These claims have been maintained and established as far west as the river Mississippi, by the sword. The title to a vast portion of the lands we now hold, originates in them. It is not for the Courts of this country to question the validity of this title, or to sustain one which is incompatible with it. . . .

The title by conquest is acquired and maintained by

16

force. The conqueror prescribes its limits. Humanity, however, acting on public opinion, has established, as a general rule, that the conquered shall not be wantonly oppressed, and that their condition shall remain as eligible as is compatible with the objects of the conquest. Most usually, they are incorporated with the victorious nation, and become subjects or citizens of the government with which they are connected. The new and old members of the society mingle with each other; the distinction between them is gradually lost, and they make one people. . . .When the conquest is complete, and the conquered inhabitants can be blended with the conquerors, or safely governed as a distinct people, public opinion, which not even the conqueror can disregard, imposes these restraints upon him; and he cannot neglect them without injury to his fame, and hazard to his power. But the tribes of Indians inhabiting this country were fierce savages, whose occupation was war, and whose subsistence was drawn chiefly from the forest. To leave them in possession of their country, was to leave the country a wilderness; to govern them as a distinct people, was impossible, because they were as brave and as high spirited as they were fierce, and were ready to repel by arms every attempt on their independence. What was the inevitable consequence of this state of things? The Europeans were under the necessity either of abandoning the country, and relinquishing their pompous claims to it, or of enforcing those claims by the sword, and by the adoption of principles adapted to the condition of a people with whom it was impossible to mix, and who could not be governed as a distinct society, or of remaining in their neighbourhood, and exposing themselves and their families to the perpetual hazard of being massacred. Frequent and bloody wars, in which the whites were not always the aggressors, unavoidably ensued. European policy, numbers, and skill, prevailed. As the white population advanced, that of the Indians necessarily receded. The country in the immediate neighbourhood of

17

agriculturists became unfit for them. The game fled into thicker and more unbroken forests, and the Indians followed. The soil, to which the crown originally claimed title, being no longer occupied by its ancient inhabitants, was parcelled out according to the will of the sovereign power, and taken possession of by persons who claimed immediately from the crown, or mediately, through its grantees or deputies. That law which regulates, and ought to regulate in general, the relations between the conqueror and conquered, was incapable of application to a people under such circumstances. The resort to some new and different rule, better adapted to the actual state of things, was unavoidable. Every rule which can be suggested will be found to be attended with great difficulty. However extravagant the pretension of converting the discovery of an inhabited country into conquest may appear; if the principle has been asserted in the first instance, and afterwards sustained; if a country has been acquired and held under it; if the property of the great mass of the community originates in it, it becomes the law of the land, and cannot be questioned. So, too, with respect to the concomitant principle, that the Indian inhabitants are to be considered merely as occupants, to be protected, indeed, while in peace, in the possession of their lands, but to be deemed incapable of transferring the absolute title to others. However this restriction may be opposed to natural right, and to the usages of civilized nations, yet, if it be indispensable to that system under which the country has been settled, and be adapted to the actual condition of the two people, it may, perhaps, be supported by reason, and certainly cannot be rejected by Courts of justice. The proclamation issued by the King of Great Britain, in 1763, has been considered, and, we think, with reason, as constituting an additional objection to the title of the plaintiffs. By that proclamation, the crown reserved under its own dominion and protection, for the use of the Indians, "all the land and territories lying to the westward of the sources of the rivers which fall into the sea from the west and northwest," and strictly forbade all British subjects from making any purchases or settlements whatever, or taking possession of the reserved lands. It has been contended, that, in this proclamation, the king transcended his constitutional powers; and the case of *Campbell v. Hall*, (reported by Cowper,) is relied on to support this position. It is supposed to be a principle of universal law, that, if an uninhabited country be discovered by a number of individuals, who acknowledge no connexion with, and owe no allegiance to, any government whatever, the country becomes the property of the discoverers, so far at least as they can use it. They acquire a title in common. The title of the whole land is in the whole society. It is to be divided and parcelled out according to the will of the society, expressed by the whole body, or by that organ which is authorized by the whole to express it.

Doctrine of Discovery

If the discovery be made, and possession of the country be taken, under the authority of an existing government, which is acknowledged by the emigrants, it is supposed to be equally well settled, that the discovery is made for the whole nation, that the country becomes a part of the nation, and that the vacant soil is to be disposed of by that organ of the government which has the constitutional power to dispose of the national domains, by that organ in which all vacant territory is vested by law. According to the theory of the British constitution, all vacant lands are vested in the crown, as representing the nation; and the exclusive power to grant them is admitted to reside in the crown, as a branch of the royal prerogative. It has been already shown, that this principle was as fully recognised in America as in the island of Great Britain. All the lands we hold were originally granted by the crown; and the establishment of a regal government has never been considered as impairing its right to grant lands within the chartered limits of such colony. In addition to the proof of this principle, furnished by the immense grants, already mentioned, of lands lying within the chartered limits of Virginia, the continuing right of the crown to grant lands lying within that colony was always admitted. A title might be obtained, either by making an entry with the surveyor of a county, in pursuance of law, or by an order of the governor in council, who was the deputy of the king, or by an immediate grant from the crown. In Virginia, therefore, as well as elsewhere in the British dominions, the complete title of the crown to vacant lands was acknowledged. So far as respected the authority of the crown, no distinction was taken between vacant lands and lands occupied by the Indians. The title, subject only to the right of occupancy by the Indians, was admitted to be in the king, as was his right to grant that title. The lands, then, to which this proclamation referred, were lands which the king had a right to grant, or to reserve for the Indians. The authority of this proclamation, so far as it respected this continent, has never been denied, and the titles it gave to lands have always been sustained in our Courts. It has been stated, that in the memorial transmitted from the Cabinet of London to that of Versailles, during the controversy between the two nations, respecting boundary, which took place in 1755, the Indian right to the soil is recognised. But this recognition was made with reference to their character as Indians, and for the purpose of showing that they were fixed to a particular territory. It was made for the purpose of sustaining the claim of his Britannic majesty to dominion over them. . . It has never been contended, that the Indian title amounted to nothing. Their right of possession has never been questioned. The claim of government extends to the complete ultimate title, charged with this right of possession, and to the exclusive power of acquiring that right. The object of the crown was to settle the seacoast of America; and when a portion of it was settled, without violating the rights of others, by persons professing their loyalty, and soliciting the royal sanction of an act, the consequences of which were ascertained to be beneficial, it would have been as unwise as ungracious to expel them from their habitations, because they had obtained the Indian title otherwise than through the agency of government.

Judgment affirmed, with costs.

The "memorial" referred to in the opinion between London and Versailles in 1755, was the French admonishing the English for attacking their ship without provocation and then the English failing to apologize and pay restitution, all tantamount to a declaration of war. Marshall references the 1755 memorial as the first official recognition of Indians in America and the right to their land. During this time the British were enticing Indians to withdraw from all relations with the French due to their ongoing conflict. The English at the time recognized the "Indian right to the soil" by seeking to determine what lands were at stake occupied by the Indians:

> pleafure. The bufinefs therefore of the Englifh governors, at this congrefs, was to afcertain the limits of the lands in difpute, reconcile the Six Nations with their nephews the Delawares, remove every caufe of mifunderftanding between the Eng- lifh and the Indians, detach thefe favages entirely from the French intereft, eftablifh a firm peace, and induce them to exert their influence in per- fuading the Twightwees to accede to this treaty.

1755 Memorial between London and Versailles and supporting documentation

By acknowledging the need to know the "limits of the land in dispute" with the Indians the British acknowledged the Indians dominion and control over the land and their right to occupy it. But the motive for the British is to defeat the French by conceding that the Indians own and control their land in order to reach agreement that they cease relations with the French.

While the acknowledgment of the Indians' "right to soil" is affirming and useful, the court's analysis uses two legal fictions to take control of the land, both diminishing sovereignty: the Indian Trust Doctrine and the "domestic dependent nations" analyses of sovereignty.

Chief Justice Marshall opens his opinion with "[C]onquest gives a title which the Courts of the conqueror cannot deny," that gives us an idea where the opinion will end – Indians' land interests will be subordinate to the U.S. land interests.

The affirming doctrine of the rights of Indians was stated in the negative, as ". . . [I]t has never been contended, that the Indian title amounted to nothing. Their right of possession has never been questioned."

What was at issue here was the title of a British citizen who had acquired his land from Indians, through the authority of the government. Without recognizing the Indians had a "right in soil" to transfer the land to the British citizen, the British citizen would hold nothing. This would extend to all of American land titles, that is, the land acquired through treaties with Indian tribes. If the court did not recognize Indian title in this individual case, then the court could not recognize any of the treaty-acquired land was legally acquired! Thus the tribes received just enough acknowledgment of their "right to soil" as was required to recognize the title that was passed to American non-Indian land title holders.

The history of the loss of land to tribes is told by Chief Justice Marshall with striking aloofness, as if he is unaware of the broken treaties, attacks on tribes, and decimating diseases brought from Europe that disposed Indians from their land.

The country in the immediate neighbourhood of
agriculturists became unfit for them. The game fled

22

into thicker and more unbroken forests, and the Indians followed. The soil, to which the crown originally claimed title, being no longer occupied by its ancient inhabitants, was parcelled out according to the will of the sovereign power, and taken possession of by persons who claimed immediately from the crown, or mediately, through its grantees or deputies.

The tribes on the East coast met with genocidal government actions, and where that failed, they used the judiciary to fine them for corrupt criminal convictions for infractions that required payment of fines in their land. If it required legislative action, the government simply uses the term "settlement" acts. Anytime the word "settlement" is used in an agreement with Indians, it means the issue is being settled by the U.S. government in their favor and to bring closure to the outstanding conflict, fair or not.

By 1790, the United States Congress passed the first federal law to stop the sale and trade of land between individuals, states and Native Americans or tribal nations. This was the 1790 Trade and Intercourse Act, and that gave the federal government exclusive control over the acquisition of Indian land through treatymaking.

After the War of 1812, conciliatory attitudes changed, and the Indian Nations were not in a strong political position now that the threat of Great Britain had subsided.

The next two cases in the trilogy involve the Cherokee Nation in Georgia in the 1830s, called the Cherokee cases. Both cases arise from the conflict over the arrest of a non-Indian minister who was being detained on questionable legal grounds. Like many American Indian law cases that followed, a case involving an individual often results in deciding a much broader legal issue that affects all tribes. That was certainly the outcome for these next two cases. Together they form the judicial interpretation for the doctrines of trust responsibility, the characterization of tribal nations as "domestic dependent nations", tribal sovereignty and the supremacy and binding nature of treaties.

The Cherokee Cases

In 1831 and 1832, two cases involving Cherokee Nation and Georgia state jurisdictional issues came before the U.S. Supreme Court. The first case was initiated by an Indian tribe, the Cherokee Nation which brought this case before the U.S. Supreme Court[3] as the court of original jurisdiction for resolving legal disputes between sovereigns. To achieve this kind of original jurisdiction in the U.S. Supreme Court, the Cherokee Nation had to be considered a "foreign nation" as defined in Art. III, § 2 of the U.S. Constitution.

However, the Cherokee Nation lost their argument for jurisdiction, with Justice Marshall finding them to be "domestic dependent nations" although capable of self-government, but *not* a "foreign government".[4] This left the Cherokees with no judicial forum, since their dispute was with the state of Georgia, and represented a major blow to Indian tribal sovereignty.

Members of the Cherokee Nation appeared in the U.S. Supreme Court to watch the oral argument by their attorneys, William Wirt and John Sergeant. One newspaper reported that the Indians looked "intelligent and respectable," which tended to dispute the description of Indians as "savages" and "uncivilized". It was also reported that one member of the Cherokee delegation "shed tears copiously during Mr. Wirt's address" at points where he highlighted injustices and unfairness.

The state of Georgia did not show up to court to make their point that they were not subject to the jurisdiction of the court and that tribes did not have standing to be heard as a party before the U.S. Supreme court which has exclusive jurisdiction over cases between states and foreign states. Article III of the Constitution extends the judicial power to

---

[3] <u>Cherokee Nation v. Georgia</u>, 30 U.S. (5 Pet.) 1 (1831).
[4] U.S. Const., Art. III

25

Controversies between two or more States, between a
State and Citizens of another State . . ., and between
a State . . . and foreign States, Citizens or Subjects.

The Judiciary Act of 1789 clarified that the Supreme Court exclusive original jurisdiction.

The Cherokee cases together establish the doctrines of trust responsibility, the legal constitutional status of Indian nations as "domestic dependent nations" and issues of sovereignty and the legal recognition of treaties.

The following case, Cherokee Nation v. Georgia comes after a previous case where the U.S. Supreme Court had issued a writ of error (intervened to stop an execution) over a Cherokee individual (Corn Tassell) convicted of a murder between two tribal members within the jurisdiction of the Cherokee Nation over which Georgia did not have jurisdiction. The Georgia governor, George Gilmer, pronounced to the Georgia legislature that "orders from the Supreme Court . . . will be disregarded." The Legislature followed with a Resolution that "his Excellency, the governor, be . . . and every other officer of this state, is hereby requested and enjoined to disregard any and every mandate." Then Georgia proceeded to execute Corn Tassell.

The Cherokee Nation tried to peacefully resolve these differences including an effort to lobby politicians in Washington. Elias Boudinot, wrote an editorial for the Cherokee Phoenix, the Nation's newspaper, that they were seeking to be heard before the U.S. Supreme Court and that Georgia should do the same. He wrote,

> "We will merely say that if the highest judicial tribunal in the land will not sustain our rights and treaties we give up and quit our murmurings. . ." [Elias Boudinot, Editorial, Cherokee Phoenix, July 3, 1980.]

The Cherokee delegation was represented by William Wirt and Daniel Webster before the U.S. Supreme Court in a case that was intended to show that the Cherokee Nation was a sovereign nation and that treaties were the law. [Rennard Strickland, "The Tribal Struggle for Indian Sovereignty: The Story of the Cherokee Cases," Eds. Goldberg, Washburn and Frickey, Indian Law Stories (2011)].

The excerpt is edited and is about one-third of the original text, but highlights the analysis of sovereignty and the recognition of treaties. The logic of the Cherokee Nation's argument was this: (1) under the Constitution, Art. III, the Cherokees are either a state or a foreign nation; and (2) they are not a state; (3) therefore, they are a foreign nation.5

Cherokee Nation v. Georgia
30 U.S. (5 Pet.) 1 (1831)

January Term, 1831
Justice John Marshall

Page 2

THIS case came before the court on a motion on behalf of the Cherokee nation of Indians for a subpoena, and for an injunction, to restrain the state of Georgia, the governor, attorney-general, judges, justices of the peace, sheriffs, deputy sheriffs, constables, and others the officers, agents, and servants of that state, from executing and enforcing the laws of Georgia or any of these laws, or serving process, or doing any thing towards the execution or enforcement of those laws, within the Cherokee territory, as

---

5 Rennard Strickland, "The Tribal Struggle for Indian Sovereignty: The Story of the Cherokee Cases," Eds. Goldberg, Washburn and Frickey, Indian Law Stories (2011)].

designated by treaty between the United States and the Cherokee nation.

. . .

The bill set forth the complainants to be 'the Cherokee nation of Indians, a foreign state, not owing allegiance to the United States, nor to any state of this union, nor to any prince, potentate or state, other than their own.' 'That from time immemorial the Cherokee nation have composed a sovereign and independent state, and in this character have been repeatedly recognized, and still stand recognized by the United States, in the various treaties subsisting between their nation and the United States.' That the Cherokees were the occupants and owners of the territory in which they now reside, before the first approach of the white men of Europe to the western continent; 'deriving their title from the Great Spirit, who is the common father of the human family, and to whom the whole earth belongs.' Composing the Cherokee nation, they and their ancestors have been and are the sole and exclusive masters of this territory, governed by their own laws, usages, and customs.

The bill states the grant, by a charter in 1732, of the country on this continent lying between the Savannah and Alatahama rivers, by George the Second, 'monarch of several islands on the eastern coast of the Atlantic,' the same country being then in the ownership of several distinct, sovereign, and independent nations of Indians, and amongst them the Cherokee nation.

The foundation of this charter, the bill states is asserted to be the right of *discovery* to the territory granted; a ship manned by the subjects of the king having, 'about two centuries and a half before, sailed along the coast of the western hemisphere, from the fifty-sixth to the thirty-eighth degree of north latitude, and looked upon the face of that coast without even landing on any part of it.' This right, as affecting the right of the Indian nation, the bill denies; and asserts that the whole length to which the right of discovery is claimed to extend among European nations is to give to the first discoverer the prior and exclusive right to purchase these lands from the Indian proprietors, against all other European sovereigns: to which principle the Indians have never assented; and which they deny to be a principle of the natural law of nations, or obligatory on them.

The bill alleges, that it never was claimed under the charter of George the Second, that the grantees had a right to disturb the self government of the Indians who were in possession of the country; and that, on the contrary, treaties were made by the first adventurers with the Indians, by which a part of the territory was acquired by them for a valuable consideration; and no pretension was ever made to set up the British laws in the country owned by the Indians. That various treaties have been, from time to time, made between the British colony in Georgia; between the state of Georgia, before her confederation with the other states; between the confederate states afterwards; and, finally, between the United States under their present constitution, and the Cherokee nation, as well as other nations of Indians: in all of which the Cherokee nation, and the other nations have been recognized as sovereign and independent states; possessing both the exclusive right to their territory, and the exclusive right of self government within that territory. That the various proceedings from time to time had by the congress of the United States under the articles of their confederation, as well as under the present constitution of the United States, in relation to the subject of the Indian nations; confirm the same view of the subject.

. . .

By those treaties the bill asserts the Cherokee nation of Indians are acknowledged and treated with as sovereign and independent states, within the boundary arranged by those treaties: and that the complainants are, within the boundary established by the treaty of 1719, sovereign and independent; with the right of self government, without any right of interference with the same on the part of any state of the United States. The bill calls the attention of the court to the particular provisions of those treaties, 'for the purpose of verifying the truth of the general principles deduced from them.'

The bill alleges, from the earliest intercourse between the United States and the Cherokee nation, an ardent desire has been evinced by the United States to lead the Cherokees to a greater degree of civilization
. . .

The bill claims for the Cherokee nation the benefit of the provision in the constitution; that treaties are the supreme law of the land; and all judges are bound thereby: of the declaration in the constitution, ... That congress have, in execution of this power, passed various acts, and among others the act of 1802, 'to regulate trade and intercourse with the Indian tribes, and to preserve peace on the frontiers.' The objects of these acts are to consecrate the Indian boundary as arranged by the treaties; and they contain clear recognitions of the sovereignty of the Indians, and of their exclusive right to give and to execute the law within that boundary.

The bill proceeds to state that, in violation of these treaties, of the constitution of the United States, and of the act of congress of 1802, the state of Georgia, at a session of her legislature held in December in the year 1828, passed an act, which received the assent of the governor of that state on the twentieth day of that month and year; entitled, 'an act to add the territory lying within this state and occupied by the Cherokee Indians, to the counties of Carroll, De Kalb, Gwinett, Hall, and Habersham, and to extend the laws of this state over the same, and for other purposes.'
. . .

The effect of these laws, and their purposes, are stated to be, to parcel out the territory of the Cherokees; to extend all the laws of Georgia over the same; to abolish the

30

Cherokee laws, and to deprive the Cherokees of the
protection of their laws; to prevent them, as individuals, from
enrolling for emigration, under the penalty of indictment
before the state courts of Georgia; to make it murder in the
officers of the Cherokee government to inflict the sentence
of death in conformity with the Cherokee laws, subjecting
them all to indictment therefor, and death by hanging;
extending the jurisdiction of the justices of the peace of
Georgia into the Cherokee territory, and authorising the
calling out of the militia of Georgia to enforce the process;
and finally, declaring that no Indian, or descendant of any
Indian, residing within the Cherokee nation of Indians, shall
be deemed a competent witness in any court of the state of
Georgia, in which a white person may be a party, except such
white person resides within the said nation.

. . .

These proceedings it is alleged are wholly inconsistent
with equity and good conscience, tend to the manifest wrong
of the complainants; and violate the faith of the treaties to
which Georgia and the United States are parties, and of the
constitution of the United States. These wrongs are of a
character wholly irremediable by the common law; and these
complainants are wholly without remedy of any kind, except
by the interposition of this honourable court.

The bill avers that this court has, by the constitution
and laws of the United States, original jurisdiction of
controversies between a state and a foreign state, without any
restriction as to the nature of the controversy; that, by the
constitution, treaties are the supreme law of the land. That as
a foreign state, the complainants claim the exercise of the
powers of the court of protect them in their rights, and that
the laws of Georgia, which interfere with their rights and
property, shall be declared void, and their execution be
perpetually enjoined.

. . .

31

The complainants beg leave farther to state, that the legislature of the state of Georgia, at the same session, passed the following laws, which have received the sanction of the governor of the state.

'An act to authorize the survey and disposition of lands within the limits of Georgia, in the occupancy of the Cherokee tribe of Indians, and all other unlocated lands within the limits of the said state, claimed as Creek land; and to authorize the governor to call out the military force to protect surveyors in the discharge of their duties: and to provide for the punishment of persons who may prevent, or attempt to prevent any surveyor from performing his duties, as pointed out by this act, or who shall wilfully cut down or deface any marked trees, or remove any land-marks which may be made in pursuance of this act; and to protect the Indians in the peaceable possession of their improvements, and of the lots on which the same may be situate.'

Under this law it is stated that the lands within the boundary of the Cherokee territory are to be surveyed, and to be distributed by lottery among the people of Georgia.

. . .

Is the Cherokee nation a foreign state in the sense in which that term is used in the constitution?

13

The counsel for the plaintiffs have maintained the affirmative of this proposition with great earnestness and ability. So much of the argument as was intended to prove the character of the Cherokees as a state, as a distinct political society, separated from others, capable of managing its own affairs and governing itself, has, in the opinion of a majority of the judges, been completely successful. They have been uniformly treated as a state from the settlement of our country. The numerous treaties made with them by the United States recognize them as a people capable of maintaining the relations of peace and war, of being responsible in their political character for any violation of their engagements, or for any aggression committed on the citizens of the United States by any individual of their community. Laws have been enacted in the spirit of these treaties. The acts of our government plainly recognize the Cherokee nation as a state, and the courts are bound by those acts.

14

A question of much more difficulty remains. Do the Cherokees constitute a foreign state in the sense of the constitution?

15

The counsel have shown conclusively that they are not a state of the union, and have insisted that individually they are aliens, not owing allegiance to the United States. An aggregate of aliens composing a state must, they say, be a foreign state. Each individual being foreign, the whole must be foreign.

16

This argument is imposing, but we must examine it more closely before we yield to it. The condition of the Indians in relation to the United States is perhaps unlike that of any other two people in existence. In the general, nations not owing a common allegiance are foreign to each other. The term *foreign nation* is, with strict propriety, applicable by either to the other. But the relation of the Indians to the United States is marked by peculiar and cardinal distinctions which exist no where else.

17

The Indian territory is admitted to compose a part of the United States. In all our maps, geographical treatises, histories, and laws, it is so considered. In all our intercourse with foreign nations, in our commercial regulations, in any attempt at intercourse between Indians and foreign nations, they are considered as within the jurisdictional limits of the United States, subject to many of those restraints which are imposed upon our own citizens. They acknowledge themselves in their treaties to be under the protection of the United States; they admit that the United States shall have the sole and exclusive right of regulating the trade with them, and managing all their affairs as they think proper; and the Cherokees in particular were allowed by the treaty of Hopewell, which preceded the constitution, 'to send a deputy of their choice, whenever they think fit, to congress.

. . .

18

Though the Indians are acknowledged to have an unquestionable, and, heretofore, unquestioned right to the lands they occupy, until that right shall be extinguished by a voluntary cession to our government; yet it may well be doubted whether those tribes which reside within the acknowledged boundaries of the United States can, with strict accuracy, be denominated foreign nations. They may, more correctly, perhaps, be denominated <u>domestic dependent nations.</u> They occupy a territory to which we assert a title independent of their will, which must take effect in point of possession when their right of possession ceases. Meanwhile they are in a state of pupilage. Their relation to the United States resembles that of a ward to his guardian.

19

They look to our government for protection; rely upon its kindness and its power; appeal to it for relief to their wants; and address the president as their great father. They and their country are considered by foreign nations, as well as by ourselves, as being so completely under the sovereignty and dominion of the United States, that any attempt to acquire their lands, or to form a political connexion with them, would be considered by all as an invasion of our territory, and an act of hostility.

. . .

40

There are great difficulties hanging over the question, whether they can be considered as states under the judiciary article of the constitution. 1. They never have been recognized as holding sovereignty over the territory they occupy. It is in vain now to inquire into the sufficiency of the principle, that <u>discovery</u> gave the right of dominion over the country discovered. When the populous and civilized nations beyond the Cape of Good Hope were visited, the <u>right of discovery</u> was made the ground of an exclusive right to their trade, and confined to that limit. When the eastern coast of this continent, and especially the part we inhabit, was discovered, finding it occupied by a race of hunters, connected in society by scarcely a semblance of organic government; the right was extended to the absolute appropriation of the territory, the annexation of it to the domain of the discoverer. It cannot be questioned that the right of sovereignty, as well as soil, was notoriously asserted and exercised by the European discoverers. From that source we derive our rights, and there is not an instance of a cession of land from an Indian nation, in which the right of sovereignty is mentioned as a part of the matter ceded. 41

It may be suggested that they were uniformly cessions of land without inhabitants; and, therefore, words competent to make a cession of sovereignty were unnecessary.

. . .

And almost every attribute of sovereignty is renounced by them in that very treaty. They acknowledge themselves to be under the sole and exclusive protection of the United States. They receive the territory allotted to them as a boon, from a master or conqueror; the right of punishing intruders into that territory is conceded, not asserted as a right; and the sole and exclusive right of regulating their trade and managing all their affairs in such manner as the government of the United States shall think proper; amounting in terms to a relinquishment of all power, legislative, executive and judicial to the United States

. . .

. From that time Great Britain considered them as her subjects whenever she chose to claim their allegiance; and their country as hers, both in soil and sovereignty. All the forbearance exercised towards them was considered as voluntary; and as their trade was more valuable to her than their territory, for that reason, and not from any supposed want of right to extend her laws over them, did she abstain from doing so.

55

And, thirdly, by what attributes is the Cherokee nation identified with other states?

56

The right of sovereignty was expressly assumed by Great Britain over their country at the first taking possession of it; and has never since been recognized as in them, otherwise than as dependent upon the will of a superior.

57

The right of legislation is in terms conceded to congress by the treaty of Hopewell, whenever they choose to exercise it. And the right of soil is held by the feeble tenure of hunting grounds, and acknowledged on all hands subject to a restriction to sell to no one but the United States, and for no use but that of Georgia.

58

They have in Europe sovereign and demi-sovereign states and states of doubtful sovereignty. But this state, if it be a state, is still a grade below them all: for not to be able to alienate without permission of the remainder-man or lord, places them in a state of feudal dependence.

59

However, I will enlarge no more upon this point; because I believe, in one view and in one only, if at all, they are or may be deemed a state, though not a sovereign state, at least while they occupy a country within our limits. Their condition is something like that of the Israelites, when inhabiting the deserts. Though without land that they can call

theirs in the sense of property, their right of personal self government has never been taken from them; and such a form of government may exist though the land occupied be in fact that of another. The right to expel them may exist in that other, but the alternative of departing and retaining the right of self government may exist in them. And such they certainly do possess; it has never been questioned, nor any attempt made at subjugating them as a people, or restraining their personal liberty except as to their land and trade.
60

But in no sense can they be deemed a foreign state, under the judiciary article.
76

But this argument cannot bear the test of principle. For the jurisdiction of a country may be exercised over her citizens wherever they are, in right of their allegiance; as it has been in the instance of punishing offences committed against the Indians. And, also, both under the constitution and the treaty of Hopewell, the power of congress extends to regulating their trade, necessarily within their limits. But this cannot sanction the exercise of jurisdiction beyond the policy of the acts themselves; which are altogether penal in their provisions.
77

I vote for rejecting the motion.

78
Mr Justice BALDWIN.

79

As jurisdiction is the first question which must arise in every cause, I have confined my examination of this, entirely to that point, and that branch of it which relates to the capacity of the plaintiffs to ask the interposition of this court. I concur in the opinion of the court in dismissing the bill, but not for the reasons assigned.

37

80

In my opinion there is no plaintiff in this suit; and this opinion precludes any examination into the merits of the bill, or the weight of any minor objections. My judgment stops me at the threshold, and forbids me to examine into the acts complained of.

. . .

82

My view of the plaintiffs being a sovereign independent nation or foreign state, within the meaning of the constitution, applies to all the tribes with whom the Unites States have held treaties: for if one is a foreign nation or state, all others in like condition must be so in their aggregate capacity; and each of their subjects or citizens, aliens, capable of suing in the circuit courts. This case then is the case of the countless tribes, who occupy tracts of our vast domain; who, in their collective and individual characters, as states or aliens, will rush to the federal courts in endless controversies, growing out of the laws of the states or of congress.

83

In the spirit of the maxim *obsta principiis*, I shall first proceed to the consideration of the proceedings of the old congress, from the commencement of the revolution up to the adoption of the constitution; so as to ascertain whether the Indians were considered and treated with as tribes of savages, or independent nations, foreign states on an equality with any other foreign state or nation; and whether Indian affairs were viewed as those of foreign *nations*, and in connection with this view, refer to the acts of the federal government on the same subject.

. . .

92

      After accepting the cessions of the soil and jurisdiction of the western territory, and resolving to form a temporary government, and create new, free, sovereign, and independent states, congress resolved, in March 1785, to hold a treaty with the western Indians. They gave instructions to the commissioners in strict conformity with their preceding resolutions, both of which were wholly incompatible with the national or sovereign character of the Indians with whom they were about to treat. . . .

. . .

96

      In considering the bearing of the constitution on their rights, it must be borne in mind, that a majority of the states represented in the convention had ceded to the United States the soil and jurisdiction of their western lands, or claimed it to be remaining in themselves; that congress asserted as to the ceded, and the states as to the unceded territory, their right to the soil absolutely and the dominion in full sovereignty, within their respective limits, subject only to Indian occupancy, not as foreign states or nations, but as dependent on and appendant to the state governments: that before the convention acted, congress had erected a government in the north western territory containing numerous and powerful nations or tribes of Indians, whose jurisdiction was continued and whose sovereignty was overturned, if it ever existed, except by permission of the states or congress, by ordaining that the territorial laws should extend over the whole district; and directing divisions for the execution of civil and criminal process in every part; that the Cherokees were then dependants, having given up all their affairs to the regulation and management of congress, and that all the regulations of congress, over Indian affairs were then in force over an immense territory, under a solemn pledge to the inhabitants, that whenever their population and circumstances would admit they should form constitutions and become free, sovereign and independent states on equal footing with the old component members of the confederation; that by the existing regulations and treaties, the Indian tenure to their lands was their allotment as hunting grounds without the power of alienation, that the right of occupancy was not individual, that the Indians were forbidden all trade or intercourse with any person not licensed or at a post not designated by regulation, that Indian affairs formed no part of the foreign concerns of the government, and that though they were permitted to regulate their internal affairs in their own way, it was not by any inherent right acknowledged by congress or reserved by treaty, but because congress did not think proper to exercise the sole and exclusive right, declared and asserted in all their regulations from 1775 to 1788, in the articles of confederation, in the ordinance of 1787 and the proclamation of 1788; which the plaintiffs solemnly recognized and expressly granted by the treaty of Hopewell in 1785, as conferred on congress to be exercised as they should think proper.

97

  To correctly understand the constitution, then, we must read it with reference to this well known existing state of our relations with the Indians; the United States asserting the right of soil, sovereignty, and jurisdiction, in full dominion; the Indians oecupant, of allotted hunting grounds.
. . .

101

  Guided by these principles, I come to consider the third clause of the second section of the first article of the constitution; which provides for the apportionment of representatives, and direct taxes 'among the several states which may be included within this union, according to their respective numbers, *excluding Indians not taxed.*' This clause embraces not only the old but the new states to be formed out of the territory of the United States, pursuant to the resolutions and ordinances of the old congress, and the conditions of the cession from the states, or which might arise by the division of the old. If the clause excluding Indians not taxed had not been inserted, or should be stricken out, the whole free Indian population of all the states would be included in the federal numbers, coextensively with the boundaries of all the states, included in this union. The insertion of this clause conveys a clear definite declaration that there were no independent sovereign nations or states, foreign or domestic, within their boundaries, which should exclude them from the federal enumeration, or any bodies or communities within the states, excluded from the action of the federal constitution unless by the use of express words of exclusion.

. . .

103

The third clause of the eighth article shows most distinctly the sense of the convention in authorising congress to regulate commerce with the Indian tribes. The character of the Indian communities had been settled by many years of uniform usage under the old government: characterized by the name of nations, towns, villages, tribes, head men and warriors, as the writers of resolutions or treaties might fancy; governed by no settled rule, and applying the word nation to the Catawbas as well as the Cherokees. The framers of the constitution have thought proper to define their meaning to be, that they were not foreign nations nor states of the union, but Indian tribes; thus declaring the sense in which they should be considered under the constitution, which refers to them as tribes only, in this clause. I cannot strike these words from the book; or construe Indian tribes in this part of the constitution to mean a sovereign state under the first clause of the second section of the third article. It would be taking very great liberty in the exposition of a fundamental law, to bring the Indians under the action of the legislative power as tribes, and of the judicial, as foreign states. The power conferred to regulate commerce with the Indian tribes, is the same given to the old congress by the ninth article of the old confederation, 'to regulate trade with the Indians.' The raising the word 'trade' to the dignity of commerce, regulatingit with Indians or Indian tribes, is only a change of words. Mere phraseology cannot make Indians nations, or Indian tribes foreign states.

. . .

Foreign states cannot be created by judicial construction; Indian sovereignty cannot be roused from its long slumber, and awakened to action by our fiat. I find no acknowledgement of it by the legislative or executive power. Till they have done so, I can stretch forth no arm for their relief without violating the constitution. I say this with great deference to those from whom I dissent; but my judgment tells me, I have no power to act, and imperious duty compels me to stop at the portal, unless I can find some authority in the judgments of this court, to which I may surrender my own.

. . .

It will be a declaration, in my deliberate judgment, that the sovereign power of the people of the United States and union must hereafter remain incapable of action over territory to which their rights in full dominion have been asserted with the most rigorous authority, and bow to a jurisdiction hitherto unknown, unacknowledged by any department of the government; denied by all through all time; unclaimed till now; and now declared to have been called into exercise, not by any change in our constitution, the laws of the union or the states; but pre-existent and paramount over the supreme law of the land.

118
Mr. Justice THOMPSON, dissenting.

119

Entertaining different views of the questions now before us in this case, and having arrived at a conclusion different from that of a majority of the court, and considering the importance of the case and the constitutional principle involved in it; I shall proceed, with all due respect for the opinion of others, to assign the reasons upon which my own has been formed.

120

In the opinion pronounced by the court, the merits of the controversy between the state of Georgia and the Cherokee Indians have not been taken into consideration. The denial of the application for an injunction has been placed solely on the ground of want of jurisdiction in this court to grant the relief prayed for. It became, therefore, unnecessary to inquire into the merits of the case. But thinking as I do that the court has jurisdiction of the case, and may grant relief, at least in part; it may become necessary for me, in the course of my opinion, to glance at the merits of the controversy; which I shall, however, do very briefly, as it is important so far as relates to the present application.

. . .But believing as I do, that relief to some extent falls properly under judicial cognizance, I shall proceed to the examination of the case under the following heads.

123

1. Is the Cherokee nation of Indians a competent party to sue in this court?2. Is a sufficient case made out in the bill, to warrant this court in granting any relief?

124

3. Is an injunction the fit and appropriate relief?

43

125

1. By the constitution of the United States it is declared (Art. 3, § 2), that the judicial power shall extend to all cases in law and equity, arising under this constitution, the laws of the United States, and treaties made or which shall be made under their authority; &c. to controversies between two or more states, &c. and between a state or the citizens thereof; and foreign states, citizens or subjects.

126

The controversy in the present case is alleged to be between a foreign state, and one of the states of the union; and does not, therefore, come within the eleventh amendment of the constitution, which declares that the judicial power of the United States, shall not be construed to extend to any suit in law or equity commenced or prosecuted against one of the United States by citizens of another state, or by citizens or subjects of any foreign state. This amendment does not, therefore, extend to suits prosecuted against one of the United States by a foreign state. The constitution further provides, that in all cases where a state shall be a party, the supreme court shall have original jurisdiction. Under these provisions in the constitution, the complainants have filed their bill in this court, in the character of a foreign state, against the state of Georgia; praying an injunction to restrain that state from committing various alleged violations of the property of the nation, claimed under the laws of the United States, and treaties made with the Cherokee nation.

127

That a state of this union may be sued by a foreign state, when a proper case exists and is presented, is too plainly and expressly declared in the constitution to admit of doubt; and the first inquiry is, whether the Cherokee nation is a foreign state within the sense and meaning of the constitution.

128

The terms *state* and *nation* are used in the law of nations, as well as in common parlance, as importing the same thing; and imply a body of men, united together, to procure their mutual safety and advantage by means of their union. Such a society has its affairs and interests to manage; it deliberates, and takes resolutions in common, and thus becomes a moral person, having an understanding and a will peculiar to itself, and is susceptible of obligations and laws. Vattel, 1. Nations being composed of men naturally free and independent, and who, before the establishment of civil societies, live together in the state of nature, nations or sovereign states; are to be considered as so many free persons, living together in a state of nature. Vattel 2, § 4. Every nation that governs itself, under what form soever, without any dependence on a foreign power, is a sovereign state. Its rights are naturally the same as those of any other state. Such are moral persons who live together in a natural society, under the law of nations. It is sufficient if it be really sovereign and independent: that is, it must govern itself by its own authority and laws. We ought, therefore, to reckon in the number of sovereigns those states that have bound themselves to another more powerful, although by an unequal alliance. The conditions of these unequal alliances may be infinitely varied; but whatever they are, provided the inferior ally reserves to itself the sovereignty or the right to govern its own body, it ought to be considered an independent state. Consequently, a weak state, that, in order to provide for its safety, places itself under the protection of a more powerful one, without stripping itself of the right of government and sovereignty, does not cease on this account to be placed among the sovereigns who acknowledge no other power. Tributary and feudatory states do not thereby

45

cease to be sovereign and independent states, so long as self government, and sovereign and independent authority is left in the administration of the state. Vattel, c. 1, pp. 16, 17.

129

Testing the character and condition of the Cherokee Indians by these rules, it is not perceived how it is possible to escape the conclusion, that they form a sovereign state. They have always been dealt with as such by the government of the United States; both before and since the adoption of the present constitution. They have been admitted and treated as a people governed solely and exclusively by their own laws, usages, and customs within their own territory, claiming and exercising exclusive dominion over the same; yielding up by treaty, from time to time, portions of their land, but still claiming absolute sovereignty and self government over what remained unsold. And this has been the light in which they have, until recently, been considered from the earliest settlement of the country by the white people. And indeed, I do not understand it is denied by a majority of the court, that the Cherokee Indians form a sovereign state according to the doctrine of the law of nations; but that, although a sovereign state, they are not considered a foreign state within the meaning of the constitution.

130

Whether the Cherokee Indians are to be considered a foreign state or not, is a point on which we cannot expect to discover much light from the law of nations. We must derive this knowledge chiefly from the practice of our own government, and the light in which the nation has been viewed and treated by it.

131

That numerous tribes of Indians, and among others the Cherokee nation, occupied many parts of this country long before the discovery by Europeans, is abundantly established by history; and it is not denied but that the Cherokee nation occupied the territory now claimed by them long before that period. It does not fall within the scope and object of the present inquiry to go into a critical examination of the nature and extent of the rights growing out of such occupancy, or the justice and humanity with which the Indians have been treated, or their rights respected.

132

That they are entitled to such occupancy, so long as they choose quietly and peaceably to remain upon the land, cannot be questioned. The circumstance of their original occupancy is here referred to, merely for the purpose of showing, that if these Indian communities were then, as they certainly were, nations, they must have been foreign nations, to all the world; not having any connexion, or alliance of any description, with any other power on earth. And if the Cherokees were then a foreign nation; when or how have they lost that character, and ceased to be a distinct people, and become incorporated with any other community?

133

They have never been, by conquest, reduced to the situation of subjects to any conqueror, and thereby lost their separate national existence, and the rights of self government, and become subject to the laws of the conqueror. When ever wars have taken place, they have been followed by regular treaties of peace, containing stipulations on each side according to existing circumstances; the Indian nation always preserving its distinct and separate national character. And notwithstanding we do not recognize the right of the Indians to transfer the absolute title of their lands to any other than ourselves; the right of occupancy is still admitted to remain in them, accompanied with the right of self government, according to their own usages and customs; and with the competency to act in a national capacity, although placed under the protection of the whites, and owing a qualified subjection so far as is requisite for public safety. But the principle is universally admitted, that this occupancy belongs to them as matter of right, and not by mere indulgence. They cannot be disturbed in the enjoyment of it, or deprived of it, without their free consent; or unless a just and necessary war should sanction their dispossession.

134

In this view of their situation, there is as full and complete recognition of their sovereignty, as if they were the absolute owners of the soil. The progress made in civilization by the Cherokee Indians cannot surely be considered as in any measure destroying their national or foreign character, so long as they are permitted to maintain a separate and distinct government; it is their political condition that constitutes their *foreign* character, and in that sense must the term *foreign*, be understood as used in the constitution. It can have no relation to local, geographical, or territorial position. It cannot mean a country beyond sea. Mexico or Canada is certainly to be considered a foreign country, in reference to the United States. It is the political relation in which one government or country stands to another, which constitutes it foreign to the other. The Cherokee territory being within the chartered limits of Georgia, does not affect the question. When Georgia is spoken of as a state, reference is had to its political character, and not be boundary; and it is not perceived that any absurdity or inconsistency grows out of the circumstance, that the jurisdiction and territory of the state of Georgia surround or extend on every side of the Cherokee territory. It may be inconvenient to the state, and very desirable, that the Cherokees should be removed; but it does not at all affect the political relation between Georgia and those Indians.

. . .

145

Such, however, is not the case with the Cherokee nation. It retains its usages and customs and self government, greatly improved by the civilization which it has been the policy of the United States to encourage and foster among them. All negotiations carried on with the Cherokees and other Indian nations have been by way of treaty with all the formality attending the making of treaties with any foreign power. The journals of congress, from the year 1775 down to the adoption of the present constitution, abundantly establish this fact. And since that period such negotiations have been carried on by the treaty-making power, and uniformly under the denomination of treaties.

146

What is a treaty as understood in the law of nations? It is an agreement or contract between two or more nations or sovereigns, entered into by agents appointed for that purpose, and duly sanctioned by the supreme power of the respective parties. And where is the authority, either in the constitution or in the practice of the government, for making any distinction between treaties made with the Indian nations and any other foreign power? They relate to peace and war; the surrender of prisoners; the cession of territory; and the various subjects which are usually embraced in such contracts between sovereign nations.

147

A recurrence to the various treaties made, with the Indian nations and tribes in different parts of the country, will fully illustrate this view of the relation in which our government has considered the Indians as standing. It will be sufficient, however, to notice a few of the many treaties made with this Cherokee nation.

. . .

No argument can be drawn against the sovereignty of these Indian nations, from the fact of their having put themselves and their lands under the protection of the British crown: such a fact is of frequent occurrence between independent nations. One community may be bound to another by a very unequal alliance, and still be a sovereign state.

186

That the Cherokee nation of Indians have, by virtue of these treaties, an exclusive right of occupancy of the lands in question, and that the United States are bound under their guarantee, to protect the nation in the enjoyment of such occupancy; cannot, in my judgment, admit of a doubt: and that some of the laws of Georgia set out in the bill are in violation of, and in conflict with those treaties and the act of 1802, is to my mind equally clear. But a majority of the court having refused the injunction, so that no relief whatever can be granted, it would be a fruitless inquiry for me to go at large into an examination of the extent to which relief might be granted by this court, according to my own view of the case.

201

Upon the whole, I am of opinion,

202

1. That the Cherokees compose a foreign state within the sense and meaning of the constitution, and constitute a competent party of maintain a suit against the state of Georgia.

203

2. That the bill presents a case for judicial consideration, arising under the laws of the United States, and treaties made under their authority with the Cherokee nation, and which laws and treaties have been, and are threatened to

be still further violated by the laws of the state of Georgia referred to in this opinion.

204

    3. That an injunction is a fit and proper writ to be issued, to prevent the further execution of such laws, and ought therefore to be awarded.

205

    And I am authorised by my brother Story to say, that he concurs with me in this opinion.

    Normally, so much space would not be afforded a dissent, but in the next case, the logic of the dissent was the majority opinion. Although the Cherokee Nation lost in this case, they were encouraged to seek the "right" case to bring before the court that might be more likely to be found in their favor. The next case was the effort to bring another case to the U.S. Supreme Court that would establish the sovereignty of the Cherokee Nation, and prevent Georgia from taking their land and selling it through a lottery as they had planned.

    Just one year later, the U.S. Supreme Court would hear the second case that would ask the question of the Cherokee Nation's status as a sovereign and whether they could be heard before the U.S. Supreme Court. In this case, there was a question as to whether Georgia could extend the jurisdiction of its civil and criminal laws over the Cherokee Nation in ***Worcester v. Georgia***.[6] This issue was the one that had given rise to the Cherokee Nation's case, ***Cherokee Nation v. Georgia*** the previous year, but an issue that the court never reached because they decided the case on

---

    [6] In ***Worcester***, a missionary to the Cherokee Nation were appealing a criminal conviction by the state of Georgia. On this occasion, the U.S. Supreme Court simply could not avoid deciding the issue.

jurisdictional grounds ---- that the Cherokee Nation was not a foreign state and therefore could not litigate with a sovereign state in the U.S. Supreme Court under Art. III, § 2.

This time, however, the United States Supreme Court found that the Cherokee Nation, while not a nation, *was* a sovereign, and Georgia therefore had no jurisdiction in the Cherokee Nation, although it was still within the boundaries of the state.

In 1830, President Andrew Jackson signed removal legislation that was intended to open lands in the southeastern United States and extinguish Indian title on the lands of the Cherokee, Chickasaw, Choctaw, Creek and Seminole nations.[7]

It is important here to consider how tribes viewed President Andrew Jackson. In the war with the Creeks who had joined with the British, Jackson was with Junaluska, a Cherokee leader born in western North Carolina in Alabama during a meeting with a council of Creek Indians. One of the Creek Indians had a knife and started toward Jackson. Junaluska had observed this and tripped him so that he was never able to plant the knife into Jackson. For that act of saving his life, Andrew Jackson upon becoming President committed the largest official act of Native American genocide to date, against the Cherokees and the other "five civilized tribes" as they were called when he ordered their removal and the long "trail of tears" walk to Indian Country. This order was contrary to the U.S. Supreme Court Ruling in the Cherokee case that follow.

---

[7] Each Nation has their own treaties and removal history. This study focuses on the Cherokee removal because it was the one heard before the U.S. Supreme Court.

Worcester v. Georgia
31 U.S. 6 Pet. 515 515 (1832)

CERTIORARI TO THE SUPERIOR COURT FOR THE
COUNTY OF
GWINETT IN THE STATE OF GEORGIA
Justice John Marshall

To the general pledge of protection have been added
several specific pledges deemed valuable by the Indians.
Some of these restrain the citizens of the United States from
encroachments on the Cherokee country, and provide for the
punishment of intruders.

The treaties and laws of the United States
contemplate the Indian territory as completely separated from
that of the States, and provide that all intercourse with them
shall be carried on exclusively by the Government of the
Union.

The Indian nations had always been considered as
distinct, independent political communities retaining their
original natural rights as undisputed possessors of the soil,
from time immemorial, with the single exception of that
imposed by irresistible power, which excluded them from
intercourse with any other European potentate than the first
discoverer of the coast of the particular region claimed, and
this was a restriction which those European potentates
imposed on themselves, as well as on the Indians. The very
term "nation," so generally applied to them, means "a people
distinct from others." The Constitution, by declaring treaties
already made, as well as those to be made, to be the supreme
law of the land, has adopted and sanctioned the previous
treaties with the Indian nations, and consequently admits
their rank among the powers who are capable of making
treaties. The words "treaty" and "nation" are words of our
own language, selected in our diplomatic and legislative
proceedings by ourselves, having each a definite and well
understood meaning. We have applied them to Indians as we

53

have applied them to the other nations of the earth. They are applied to all in the same sense.

. . .

 The Cherokee nation, then, is a distinct community, occupying its own territory, with boundaries accurately described, in which the laws of Georgia can have no force, and which the citizens of Georgia have no right to enter but with the assent of the Cherokees themselves, or in conformity with treaties and with the acts of Congress. The whole intercourse between the United States and this nation is, by our Constitution and laws, vested in the Government of the United States.

 The act of the State of Georgia under which the plaintiff in error was prosecuted is consequently void, and the judgment a nullity.

 The acts of the Legislature of Georgia interfere forcibly with the relations established between the United States and the Cherokee Nation, the regulation of which, according to the settled principles of our Constitution, is committed exclusively to the Government of the Union. They are in direct hostility with treaties, repeated in a succession of years, which mark out the boundary that separates the Cherokee country from Georgia; guaranty to them all the land within their boundary; solemnly pledge the faith of the United States to restrain their citizens from trespassing on it; and recognise the preexisting power of the Nation to govern itself.

 They are in equal hostility with the acts of Congress for regulating this intercourse and giving effect to the treaties.

. . .

 To this indictment, the plaintiff in error pleaded specially, as follows:

"And the said Samuel A. Worcester, in his own proper person, comes and says that this Court ought not to take further cognizance of the action and prosecution aforesaid, because, he says, that on the 15th day of July in the year 1831, he was, and still is, a resident in the Cherokee Nation, and that the said supposed crime, or crimes, and each of them, were committed, if committee at all, at the town of New Echota, in the said Cherokee Nation, out of the jurisdiction of this Court, and not in the county Gwinnett, or elsewhere within the jurisdiction of this Court. And this defendant saith, that he is a citizen of the State of Vermont, one of the United States of America, and that he entered the aforesaid Cherokee Nation in the capacity of a duly authorised missionary of the American Board of Commissioners for Foreign Missions, under the authority of the President of the United States, and has not since been required by him to leave it; that he was, at the time of his arrest, engaged in preaching the gospel to the Cherokee Indians, and in translating the sacred Scriptures into their language, with the permission and approval of the said Cherokee Nation, and in accordance with the humane policy of the Government of the United States, for the civilization and improvement of the Indians, and that his residence there, for this purpose, is the residence charged in the aforesaid indictment, . . .

This plea was overruled by the court; and the jurisdiction of the Superior Court of the County of Gwinnett was sustained by the judgment of the court.

The defendant was then arraigned, and pleaded "not guilty," and the case came on for trial on the 15th of September 1831, when the jury found the defendants in the indictment guilty.

. . .

A writ of error was issued on the application of the plaintiff in error, on the 27th of October 1831, which, with the following proceedings thereon, was returned to this court.

. . .

This principle, acknowledged by all Europeans because it was the interest of all to acknowledge it, gave to the nation making the discovery, as its inevitable consequence, the sole right of acquiring the soil and of making settlements on it. It was an exclusive principle which shut out the right of competition among those who had agreed to it, not one which could annul the previous rights of those who had not agreed to it. It regulated the right given by discovery among the European discoverers, but could not affect the rights of those already in possession, either as aboriginal occupants or as occupants by virtue of a discovery made before the memory of man. It gave the exclusive right to purchase, but did not found that right on a denial of the right of the possessor to sell.

The relation between the Europeans and the natives was determined in each case by the particular government which asserted and could maintain this preemptive privilege in the particular place. The United States succeeded to all the claims of Great Britain, both territorial and political, but no attempt, so far as is known, has been made to enlarge them. So far as they existed merely in theory, or were in their nature only exclusive of the claims of other European nations, they still retain their original character, and remain dormant. So far as they have been practically exerted, they exist in fact, are understood by both parties, are asserted by the one, and admitted by the other.

. . .

The extravagant and absurd idea that the feeble settlements made on the sea coast, or the companies under whom they were made, acquired legitimate power by them to govern the people, or occupy the lands from
Page 31 U. S. 545
sea to sea did not enter the mind of any man. They were well understood to convey the title which, according to the common law of European sovereigns respecting America, they might rightfully convey, and no more. This was the exclusive right of purchasing such lands as the natives were willing to sell. The Crown could not be understood to grant

56

what the Crown did not affect to claim; nor was it so understood.

. . .

The charters contain passages showing one of their objects to be the civilization of the Indians, and their conversion to Christianity -- objects to be accomplished by conciliatory conduct and good example, not by extermination.

. . .

Is it reasonable to suppose that the Indians, who could not write and most probably could not read, who certainly were not critical judges of our language, should distinguish the word "allotted" from the words "marked out." The actual subject of contract was the dividing line between the two nations,

Page 31 U. S. 553

and their attention may very well be supposed to have been confined to that subject. When, in fact, they were ceding lands to the United States, and describing the extent of their cession, it may very well be supposed that they might not understand the term employed as indicating that, instead of granting, they were receiving lands. If the term would admit of no other signification, which is not conceded, its being misunderstood is so apparent, results so necessarily from the whole transaction, that it must, we think, be taken in the sense in which it was most obviously used.

So with respect to the words "hunting grounds." Hunting was at that time the principal occupation of the Indians, and their land was more used for that purpose than for any other. It could not, however, be supposed that any intention existed of restricting the full use of the lands they reserved.

To the United States, it could be a matter of no concern whether their whole territory was devoted to hunting grounds or whether an occasional village and an occasional corn field, interrupted, and gave some variety to the scene.

57

These terms had been used in their treaties with Great
Britain, and had never been misunderstood. They had never
been supposed to imply a right in the British government to
take their lands or to interfere with their internal government.
. . .

It is the opinion of this Court that the judgment of
the Superior Court for the County of Gwinnett, in the State
of Georgia, condemning Samuel A. Worcester to hard labour
in the penitentiary of the State of Georgia for four years was
pronounced by that Court under colour of a law which is
void, as being repugnant to the Constitution, treaties, and
laws of the
Page 31 U. S. 563
United States, and ought, therefore, to be reversed and
annulled.

Mr. Justice M'LEAN.
As this case involves principles of the highest importance,
and may lead to consequences which shall have an enduring
influence on the institutions of this country, and as there are
some points in the case on which I wish to state distinctly my
opinion, I embrace the privilege of doing so.
With the decision, just given, I concur.

At no time has the sovereignty of the country been
recognized as existing in the Indians, but they have been
always admitted to possess many of the attributes of
sovereignty. All the rights which belong to self-government
have been recognized as vested in them. Their right of
occupancy has never been questioned, but the fee in the soil
has been considered in the Government. This may be called
the right to the ultimate domain, but the Indians have a
present right of possession.
. . .

What is a treaty? The answer is it is a compact formed between two nations or communities having the right of self-government.

Is it essential that each party shall possess the same attributes of sovereignty, to give force to the treaty? This will not be pretended, for, on this ground, very few valid treaties could be formed. The only requisite is that each of the contracting parties shall possess the right of self-government and the power to perform the stipulations of the treaty. Under the Constitution, no State can enter into any treaty; and it is believed that, since its adoption, no State, under its own authority, has held a treaty with the Indians.

It must be admitted that the Indians sustain a peculiar relation to the United States. They do not constitute, as was decided at the last term, a foreign State so as to claim the right to sue in the Supreme Court of the United States; and yet, having the right of self-government, they, in some sense, form a State. In the management of their internal concerns, they are dependent on no power. They punish offences under their own laws, and, in doing so, they are responsible to no earthly tribunal. They make war and form treaties of peace. The exercise of these and other powers gives to them a distinct character as a people, and constitutes them, in some respects, a state, although they may not be admitted to possess the right of soil.

By various treaties, the Cherokees have placed themselves under the protection of the United States; they have agreed to trade with no other people, nor to invoke the protection of any other sovereignty. But such engagements do not divest
Page 31 U. S. 582
them of the right of self-government, nor destroy their capacity to enter into treaties or compacts.
Every State is more or less dependent on those which surround it, but, unless this dependence shall extend so far as to merge the political existence of the protected people into

59

that of their protectors, they may still constitute a State. They may exercise the powers not relinquished, and bind themselves as a distinct and separate community.

The language used in treaties with the Indians should never be construed to their prejudice. If words be made use of which are susceptible of a more extended meaning than their plain import, as connected with the tenor of the treaty, they should be considered as used only in the latter sense. To contend that the word "allotted," in reference to the land guarantied to the Indians in certain treaties, indicates a favour conferred, rather than a right acknowledged, would, it would seem to me, do injustice to the understanding of the parties. <u>How the words of the treaty were understood by this unlettered people, rather than their critical meaning, should form the rule of construction.</u>

The question may be asked, is no distinction to be made between a civilized and savage people? Are our Indians to be placed upon a footing with the nations of Europe, with whom we have made treaties?

The inquiry is not what station shall now be given to the Indian tribes in our country?, but what relation have they sustained to us since the commencement of our government?
. . .

After a lapse of more than forty years since treaties with the Indians have been solemnly ratified by the General Government, it is too late to deny their binding force. Have the numerous treaties which have been formed with them, and the ratifications by the President and Senate, been nothing more than an idle pageantry?

By numerous treaties with the Indian tribes, we have acquired accessions of territory of incalculable value to the Union. Except by compact, we have not even claimed a right of way through the Indian lands. We have recognised in them the right to make war. No one has ever supposed that the Indians could commit treason against the United States. We have punished them for their violation of treaties, but we have inflicted the punishment on them as a nation, and not on individual offenders among them as traitors.

In the executive, legislative, and judicial branches of our government, we have admitted, by the most solemn sanctions, the existence of the Indians as a separate and distinct people, and as being vested with rights which constitute them a State, or separate community -- not a foreign, but a domestic community -- not as belonging to the Confederacy, but as existing within it, and, of necessity, bearing to it a peculiar relation.

. . .

This state of things can only be produced by a cooperation of the State and Federal Governments. The latter has the exclusive regulation of intercourse with the Indians, and, so long as this power shall be exercised, it cannot be obstructed by the State. It is a power given by the Constitution and sanctioned by the most solemn acts of both the Federal and State governments; consequently, it cannot be abrogated at the will of a State. It is one of the powers parted with by the States and vested in the Federal Government. . . .

It has been shown that the treaties and laws referred to come within the due exercise of the constitutional powers of the Federal Government; that they remain in full force, and consequently must be considered as the supreme laws of the land. These laws throw a shield over the Cherokee Indians. They guarantied to them their rights of occupancy, of self-government, and the full enjoyment of those blessings which might be attained in their humble condition. But, by the enactments of the State of Georgia, this shield is broken in pieces -- the infant institutions of the Cherokees are abolished, and their laws annulled. Infamous punishment is denounced against them for the exercise of those rights which have been most solemnly guarantied to them by the national faith.

. . .

upon the verdict upon the plea of Not guilty afterwards
pleaded by the said Samuel A. Worcester, whereby the said
Samuel A. Worcester is sentenced to hard labour in the
penitentiary of the State of Georgia, ought to be reversed and
annulled. And this Court proceeding to render such judgment
as the said Superior Court, of the State of Georgia should
have rendered, it is further ordered and adjudged that the said
judgment of the said Superior Court be, and hereby is,
reversed and annulled, and that judgment be, and hereby is,
awarded that the special plea in bar, so as aforesaid pleaded, is
a good and sufficient plea in bar in law to the indictment
aforesaid, and that all proceedings on the said indictment do
forever surcease, and that the said Samuel A. Worcester be,
and hereby is, henceforth dismissed therefrom, and that he go
thereof quit without day. And that a special mandate do go
from this Court to the said Superior Court to carry this
judgment into execution.

———————————

     The Governor of Georgia ignored the U.S. Supreme
Court's opinion that they could not dispossess the Cherokee
Nation of the land they had been guaranteed by treaty. Even
the U.S. President, Andrew Jackson, defied the court and
provided the military and the order to forcibly remove the
Cherokee citizens from their lands. They were ordered to
leave behind their belongings, and as they left many watched
white settlers run into their homes, claim them and take all of
their belongings. It remains a historic failure of humanity,
honor and the Rule of Law on the part of our nation and a
shameful Presidential legacy that will remain the darkest cloud
over any mention or recognition of President Andrew
Jackson.
     A long, tedious federal claims commission considered
claims of losses from Cherokee citizens, who had to
document and file their individual claims of loss. But only a

fraction of the losses were paid for those claims.

This federal policy brought in the "Removal Period" which began a period of almost thirty years of the removal of many tribes from the east and southeastern United States.

Removal Period (1835-1861)

President Andrew Jackson was elected in 1830, and instituted the policy of "removal" of Indians to make way for settlement based on the grand notion of "manifest destiny", a term which was repeated in Justice Marshall's foundation trilogy of cases, although it had no legal meaning. It was an idea that white colonists were entitled to sweep across the continent taking whatever they found along the way because it was their "destiny."

Efforts to make treaties with tribes turned into coercive actions and existing treaties were amended or ignored as settlement pushed westward. Often the representatives of the Tribes who signed the treaties were not the leaders or chiefs of the Tribes, but it was sufficient for the U.S. Senate to find that it could be ratified. The policy became one of divide and conquer, and tribes were forceably removed and marched on foot and wagon to "Indian Country" during all kinds of weather resulting in the genocide of unknown numbers of Native Americans. "Indian country" was an area that today is a large part the State of Oklahoma, and parts of the State of Kansas. Thanks to a recent U.S. Supreme Court decision [*McGirt v. Oklahoma*, 591 U.S. ___ , 140 S. Ct. 2452 (2020)], it was recognized that one of these reservations was never actually extinguished and by extension all other reservations in the state of Oklahoma were never extinguished. It was a landmark case that was a criminal jurisdictional case that turned out to have far reaching consequences. Again, the conflict of one individual resulted in a decision that affected all of Indian Country and multiple

63

tribal nations and their treaty interpretations.

Also during the 1830s, the first American Indian scholar, William Apes, wrote "On Our Own Ground," challenging the massive land acquisitions in Connecticut. Eventually tribal nations in New York were able to establish illegal land transfers by the state of New York that violated the federal 1790 Trade and Intercourse Act, resulting in the confirmation of their reservation. [*County of Oneida v. Oneida Indian Nation of New York State*, 470 U.S. 226 (1985)].

Reservation Period (1861-1887)

The U.S. Civil War from 1860 to 1864 led to divisions among the Indian Nations. The Western Cherokee sided with the North, while the Southern Cherokee sided with the Southern Confederacy. The Southern Cherokee made a treaty with the Confederacy which granted them a seat in Congress as well as other concessions which would give them a greater influence over their government.

The Binding Nature of Treaties comes into Question in 1871

Crucial during this period was the end of treaty making power of the Executive Branch when the U.S. Congress passed an Act on March 3, 1871.[8] This gave all power over Indian Affairs to the U.S. Congress. No one has ever challenged the constitutionality of this statute, based on the diminishment of the President's Article II constitutional powers, and whether it is constitution remains a question. Congress delegated power to the Executive to determine who is an Indian tribe and the terms of recognition. So March 3, 1871 marks the end of treatymaking power for the President with tribes.

A case, *Two Hundred and Seven Half-Pound Papers of*

---

8 16 Stat. 566; Rev. Stat. § 2079, now contained in 25 U.S.C. § 71.

Smoking Tobacco, etc., Elias C,. Boudinot et al., vs. United States, 78 U.S. 616 (1871), resulted in determining that parts of a treaty, in this case the Cherokee Treaty of 1866, could be extinguished by the court, without the consent of the Cherokee people. The provision at issue in the treaty was article 10, that Cherokee citizens had the right to sell any product or merchandise without, "any tax thereon which is now or may be levied by the United States."

The Cherokee people had been removed under the leadership of President Andrew Jackson, to Oklahoma where they were forced to start their Nation, anew. Elias Boudinot, with his uncle, negotiated the purchase of tobacco manufacturing facilities in Missouri, which he moved to the Cherokee Nation in order to avoid the payment of taxes on the merchandise, where the products were tax-exempt according to the Cherokee Treaty of 1866. The court reasoned that domestic revenue laws would control, rather than the Treaty. Treaty making power had been ended only two months earlier, leaving the power and reliance on all Treaties, in question.

The court held that Indians could be taxed for businesses that they had on their reservation lands, although they had no representation in Congress and could not have representation, because they were not American citizens.

The federal government seized all of the tobacco and manufacturing equipment, leaving Elias Boudinot, his uncle and his tribe in financial ruin. In 1883, he sought recovery through the federal Court of Claims, a court of specific jurisdiction for claims of money against the federal government, asking for $175,000 and received $3,272.25. [See David Wilkins, *American Indian Sovereignty and the United States Supreme Court*, Univ of Texas Press (1997) pp.54-63]

The End of the Treatymaking Era

In 1879, the U.S. Congress had grown tired of funding the settlements with Indian tribes that were negotiated by the President of the United States, with Art. 2, Constitutional authority. Whether Congress could constitutionally limit a President's Article 2 power has never been challenged or reviewed by a Court. So there was no formal mechanism for the President to sign peace treaties with Tribes, now, and it was left to Congress to enact specific statutes for any Tribe that was to be recognized after 1879.

It was not until the 1960s that the Bureau of Indian Affairs was delegated the task of investigating whether a tribe was a "real" Indian tribe and could be recognized. This led to hundreds of tribes being recognized as long as they met the criteria which included a history of a relationship with the federal government, usually demonstrated with a treaty between the tribe and the federal government. Many tribes without this documentation were left unrecognized, so many states began their own recognition process for tribes that were not recognized by the federal government. This was some recognition of existing sovereignty and self-governance.

The federal recognition "criteria" process governed by published regulations has been uneven, unpredictable and political, characterized by unfairness and lack of justice for many tribes. For example, until 2019, the tribe of Pocahontas was unrecognized by the federal government. Still, the tribes that were governed by Chief Seattle, the Duwamish and Suquamish tribes, have not been recognized by the federal government, despite decades of petitions.

Today, there exists a group of federally recognized tribes and state recognized tribes in the United States and federal legislation may apply whether their status is state or federal recognition.

The Rights and Status of Individual Indians— Decolonizing the stories

Is an Indian a "person" in the Constitution?

In 1879, a federal court addressed the question, whether an Indian is a person? In the case **Standing Bear v. Crook** (1879), a Nebraska federal court held that Indians are persons for the purpose of bringing a writ of habeas corpus to hear whether their freedom should be taken.

The gravity of such a decision was evident and the trial was watched very closely, because to find that an Indian was a "person" under the law, able to challenge their confinement, could challenge the entire reservation system.

The facts of the case are the following: Standing Bear and other Poncas, left their reservation and their tribal governments to become independent of their tribe. They moved to the Omaha reservation, and were arrested by the Army General Crook, acting upon orders of the Secretary of Interior, and detained until they could be removed back to their tribe and reservation. The District Attorney who was seeking their removal, argued that the court had no jurisdiction to hear their argument to challenge their confinement, because they were not American citizens, and only American citizens were entitled to file writs of habeas corpus. The court found otherwise, holding that any person is entitled to a writ of habeas corpus. The District Attorney further challenged that argument, citing the famous **Dred Scott** decision, which held that a slave could not challenge his confinement, even in a free state, because he was not a "person" under the law.

The Omaha Daily Herald editor, T. Tibbles, was outraged by the cruelty of confinement of Standing Bear and his group, so he used his position as editor to gain attention to their plight. Finally he sought the representation of John Lee Webster, a prominent attorney and A.J. Poppleton as co-counsel. The legal issues were presented at length, but particularly facts about whether the Indians were leading "civilized" lives, rather than what was considered the primitive lifestyle of Indians. With what were inordinately long arguments, Standing Bear's attorney, John Lee Webster, opened with a six-hour argument; the United States District Attorney, Lambertson gave a five hour argument; and Poppleton finished with a four hour argument. Then the court allowed Standing Bear to speak, and his remarks were interpreted for the court. It was recorded that Standing Bear rose, extended his hand toward the Judge's Bench, and for a long period of time, stood in that position, then spoke:

> *That hand is not the color of yours, but if I pierce it, I shall feel pain. If you pierce your hand, you also feel pain. The blood that will flow from mine will be the same color as yours . I am a man. God made us both.* . . [after explaining that he wanted to return to the traditional Ponca homelands, he said:] *a man bars the passage . . . I . . .must obey his orders. If he says that I cannot pass, I cannot. The long struggle will have been in vain.* [After another long pause, he continues:] *You are that man.*[9]

Tibbles in the style of a reporter of the time, described the reaction in the court: the arresting Army General Crook leaned forward and covered his eyes with his hands, women sobbed and tears appeared on the judge's face, then the entire courtroom shouted approval of the speech.[10] The opinion of Judge Dundy is excerpted, as he addresses the lengthy arguments of the parties.

---

[9] James A. Lake, Sr., **Standing Bear! Who?**, 60 Neb. L. Rev. 451, 476 (1981).
[10] Id.

United States ex. rel. Standing Bear v. Crook
Case No. 14, 891 Circuit Court, D. Nebraska
25 F. Cas. 695 (1879)

District Judge Dundy.

During the fifteen years in which I have been engaged
in administering the laws of my country, I have never been
called upon to hear or decide a case that appealed so strongly
to my sympathy as the one now under consideration. On the
one side, we have a few of the remnants of a once numerous
and powerful, but now weak, insignificant, unlettered, and
generally despised race; on the other, we have the
representative of one of the most powerful, most enlightened,
and most Christianized nations of modern times. On the one
side, we have the representatives of this wasted race coming
into this national tribunal of ours, asking for justice and
liberty to enable them to adopt our boasted civilization, and
to pursue the arts of peace, which have made us great and
happy as a nation; on the other side, we have this
magnificent, if not magnanimous, government, resisting this
application with the determination of sending these people
back to the country which is to them less desirable than
perpetual imprisonment in their own native land. But I think
it is creditable to the heart and mind of the brave and
distinguished officer who is made respondent herein to say
that he has no sort of sympathy in the business in which he is
forced by his position to bear a part so conspicuous; and, so
far as I am individually concerned, I think it not improper to
say that, If the strongest possible sympathy could give the
relators title to freedom, they would have been restored to
liberty the moment the arguments in their behalf were closed.
No examination or further thought would then have been
necessary or expedient. But in a country where liberty is
regulated by law, something more satisfactory and enduring
than mere sympathy must furnish and constitute the rule and

69

basis of judicial action. It follows that this case must be examined and decided on principles of law, and that unless the relators are entitled to their discharge under the constitution or laws of the United States, or some treaty made pursuant thereto, they must be remanded to the custody of the officer who caused their arrest, to be returned to the Indian Territory, which they left without the consent of the government. On the 8th of April, 1879, the relators, Standing Bear and twenty-five others, during the session of the court held at that time at Lincoln, presented their petition, duly verified, praying for the allowance of a writ of habeas corpus and their final discharge from custody thereunder. The petition alleges, in substance, that the relators are Indians who have formerly belonged to the Ponca tribe of Indians, now located in the Indian Territory; that they had some time previously withdrawn from the tribe, and completely severed their tribal relations therewith, and had adopted the general habits of the whites, and were then endeavoring to maintain themselves by their own exertions, and without aid or assistance from the general government; that whilst they were thus engaged, and without being guilty of violating any of the laws of the United States, they were arrested and restrained of their liberty by order of the respondent, George Crook. The writ was issued and served on the respondent on the 8th day of April, and, the distance between the place where the writ was made returnable and the place where the relators were confined being more than twenty miles, ten days were allotted in which to make return.

On the 18th of April the writ was returned, and the authority for the arrest and detention is therein shown. The substance of the return to the writ, and the additional statement since filed, is that the relators are individual members of, and connected with, the Ponca tribe of Indians; that they had fled or escaped from a reservation situated some place within the limits of the Indian Territory -- had departed therefrom without permission from the government; and, at the request of the secretary of the interior, the general of the army had issued an order which required the respondent to arrest and return the relators to their tribe in the Indian Territory, and that, pursuant to the said order, he had caused the relators to be arrested on the Omaha Indian reservation, and that they were in his custody for the purpose of being returned to the Indian Territory. It is claimed upon the one side, and denied upon the other, that the relators had withdrawn and severed, for all time, their connection with the tribe to which they belonged; and upon this point alone was there any testimony produced by either party hereto. The other matters stated in the petition and the return to the writ are conceded to be true; so that the questions to be determined are purely questions of law. On the 8th of March, 1859, a treaty was made by the United States with the Ponca tribe of Indians, by which a certain tract of country, north of the Niobrara river and west of the Missouri, was set apart for the permanent home of the said Indians, in which the government agreed to protect them during their good behavior. But just when, or how, or why, or under what circumstances, the Indians left their reservation in Dakota and went to the Indian Territory, does not appear.

The district attorney very earnestly questions the jurisdiction of the court to issue the writ, and to hear and determine the case made herein, and has supported his theory with an argument of great ingenuity and much ability. But, nevertheless, I am of the opinion that his premises are erroneous, and his conclusions, therefore, wrong and unjust. The great respect I entertain for that officer, and the very able manner in which his views were presented, make it necessary for me to give somewhat at length the reasons which lead me to this conclusion.

The district attorney discussed at length the reasons which led to the origin of the writ of habeas corpus, and the character of the proceedings and practice in connection therewith in the parent country. It was claimed that the laws

71

of the realm limited the right to sue out this writ to the free subjects of the kingdom, and that none others came within the benefits of such beneficent laws; and, reasoning from analogy, it is claimed that none but American citizens are entitled to sue out this high prerogative writ in any of the federal courts. I have not examined the English laws regulating the suing out of the writ, nor have I thought it necessary so to do. Of this I will only observe that if the laws of England are as they are claimed to be, they will appear at a disadvantage when compared with out own. This only proves that the laws of a limited monarchy are sometimes less wise and humane than the laws of our own republic -- that whilst the parliament of Great Britain was legislating in behalf of the favored few, the congress of the United States was legislating in behalf of all mankind who come within our jurisdiction.

Section 751 of the Revised Statutes declares that "the supreme court and the circuit and district courts shall have power to issue writs of habeas corpus." Section 752 confers the power to issue writs on the judges of said courts, within their jurisdiction, and declares this to be "for the purpose of inquiry into the cause of restraint of liberty." Section 753 restricts the power, limits the jurisdiction, and defines the cases where the writ may properly issue. That may be done under this section where the prisoner "is in custody under or by color of authority of the United States, . . . or is in custody for an act done or omitted in pursuance of a law of the United States, . . . or in custody in violation of the constitution or of a law or treaty of the United States." Thus, it will be seen that when a person is in custody or deprived of his liberty under color of authority of the United States, or in violation of the constitution or laws or treaties of the United States, the federal judges have jurisdiction, and the writ can properly issue.

. . . Now, it must be borne in mind that the habeas corpus act describes applicants for the writ as "persons," or "parties," who may be entitled thereto. It nowhere describes

72

them as "citizens," nor is citizenship in any way or place made a qualification for suing out the writ, and, in the absence of express provision or necessary implication which would require the interpretation contended for by the district attorney, I should not feel justified in giving the words "person" and "party" such a narrow construction.

The most natural, and therefore most reasonable, way is to attach the same meaning to words and phrases when found in a statute that is attached to them when and where found in general use. If we do so in this instance, then the question cannot be open to serious doubt. Webster describes a person as "a living soul; a self-conscious being; a moral agent; especially a living human being; a man, woman, or child; an individual of the human race." This is comprehensive enough, it would seem, to include even an Indian. In defining certain generic terms, the first section of the Revised Statutes, declares that the word "person" includes copartnerships and corporations. On the whole, it seems to me quite evident that the comprehensive language used in this section is intended to apply to all mankind -- as well the relators as the more favored white race. This will be doing no violence to language, or to the spirit or letter of the law, nor to the intention, as it is believed, of the law-making power of the government. I must hold, then, that Indians, and consequently the relators, are "persons," such as are described by and included within the laws before quoted. It is said, however, that this is the first instance on record in which an Indian has been permitted to sue out and maintain a writ of habeas corpus in a federal court, and therefore the court must be without jurisdiction in the premises. This is a non sequitur. I confess I do not know of another instance where this has been done, but I can also say that the occasion for it perhaps has never before been so great. It may be that the Indians think it wiser and better, in the end, to resort to this peaceful process than it would be to undertake the hopeless task of redressing their own alleged wrongs by force of arms.

Returning reason, and the sad experience of others similarly situated, have taught them the folly and madness of the arbitrament of the sword. They can readily see that any serious resistance on their part would be the signal for their utter extermination. Have they not, then, chosen the wiser part by resorting to the very tribunal erected by those they claim have wronged and oppressed them? This, however, is not the tribunal of their own choice, but it is the only one into which they can lawfully go for deliverance. It cannot, therefore, be fairly said that because no Indian ever before invoked the aid of this writ in a federal court, the rightful authority to issue it does not exist. Power and authority rightfully conferred do not necessarily cease to exist in consequence of long non-user. Though much time has elapsed, and many generations have passed away, since the passage of the original habeas corpus act, from which I have quoted, it will not do to say that these Indians cannot avail themselves of its beneficent provisions simply because none of their ancestors ever sought relief thereunder.

... The reasoning advanced in support of my views, leads me to conclude:

1. an Indian is a "person" within the meaning of the laws of the United States, and has, therefore, the right to sue out a writ of habeas corpus in a federal court, or before a federal judge, in all cases where he may be confined or in custody under color of authority of the United States, or where he is restrained of liberty in violation of the constitution or laws of the United States.

2. That General George Crook, the respondent, being commander of the military department of the Platte, has the custody of the relators, under color of authority of the United States, and in violation of the laws thereof.

3. That no rightful authority exists for removing by force any of the relators to the Indian Territory, as the respondent has been directed to do.

4. That the Indians possess the inherent right of expatriation, as well as the more fortunate white race, and have the inalienable right to "life, liberty, and the pursuit of happiness," so long as they obey the laws and do not trepass on forbidden ground. And,

5. Being restrained of liberty under color of authority of the United States, and in violation of the laws thereof, the relators must be discharged from custody, and it is so ordered.

Ordered accordingly.

The court also opined that the expatriation statute to conclude that a Native American had a right to severe himself from his or her tribe forever. Because of this, the court held that the Army General was not authorized to remove Standing Bear and his group back to their tribe and reservation. The court held that they had jurisdiction to consider the writ of *habeas corpus*, and upon examination of the basis for their confinement, the court released Standing Bear and his group.

Unfortunately, perhaps given the new hope from this court's opinion on May 12, 1879; on May 13, 1879, Standing Bear's brother, Big Snake and 65 other Poncas left the Ponca reservation to visit the Cheyennes, although they had been denied permission from their federal Indian agent, William Whiteman. Big Snake was arrested, and General Sherman authorized the arrest, writing, "The release under writ of habeas corpus of the Poncas in Nebraska does not apply to any other than that specific case." After several months of confinement, Big Snake was released and returned to the Ponca reservation, only to be arrested two months later, because Whiteman feared that Big Snake might assault him. On this basis Whiteman ordered Big Snake arrested and to be confined for the remainder of his life to Fort Reno, hundreds of miles away. When Big Snake resisted the arrest, a corporal shot him in the head using a rifle.[11]

Are individual Indians governed by the criminal laws of their tribes or the state governments?

In 1883, in a highly publicized murder trial, the ability of tribes to government themselves and mete out punishments for crimes of its members would be put on a political path of degradation and reduction of sovereign power.

In *Ex Parte Crow Dog*, 109 U.S. 566 (1883), the families of the murdered Spotted Tail, and the family of Crow Dog, the murderer, met and in traditional fashion, discussed the terms of settlement and blankets and other gifts were given to the family of the victim.

A broad public outcry because of a resolution that failed to give Crow Dog the death penalty, resulted in a criminal trial. Although Spotted Tail was a favorite among the white community, Crow Dog won respect from the nation when he was released on bail, with a promise to appear for his trial. The federal agents arrested Crow Dog and took him to Deadwood, Dakota Territory, to the federal territorial court and he was tried and convicted by a federal jury.

Crow Dog convinced the marshall that he should be released to settle his affairs, and so he was released on the promise that he would return for sentencing. It was a snowy day when Crow Dog was due to report back to the Federal Marshall and all bets were that he would not appear; however out of the blizzard emerged Crow Dog, to the Federal Marshall's office at the appointed time. This was reported in the news papers and Crow Dog was a hero. At this, volunteers appeared to file a writ of Habeas corpus on his

---

[11] James A. Lake, Sr., *Standing Bear! Who?*, 60 Neb. L. Rev. 451, 492 ,fn 102 (1981).

behalf with the Supreme Court.

Ex Parte Crow Dog
Supreme Court of the United States
109 U.S. 566 (1883)

Justice Matthews delivered the opinion of the court. The petitioner is in the custody of the marshal of the United States for the Territory of Dakota, imprisoned in the jail of Lawrence County, in the First Judicial District of that Territory, under sentence of death, adjudged against him by the district court for that district, to be carried into execution January 14th, 1884. That judgment was rendered upon a conviction for the murder of an Indian of the Brule Sioux band of the Sioux nation of Indians, by the name of Sin-ta-ge-le-Scka, or in English, Spotted Tail, the prisoner also being an Indian, of the same band and nation, and the homicide having occurred as alleged in the indictment, in the Indian country, within a place and district of country under the exclusive jurisdiction of the United States and within the said judicial district. The judgment was affirmed, on a writ of error, by the Supreme Court of the Territory. It is claimed on behalf of the prisoner that the crime charged against him, and of which he stands convicted, is not an offence under the laws of the United States; that the district court had no jurisdiction to try him, and that its judgment and sentence are void. He therefore prays for a writ of habeas corpus, that he may be delivered from an imprisonment which he asserts to be illegal.

The indictment is framed upon section 5339 of the Revised Statutes. That section is found in title LXX., on the subject of crimes against the United States, and in chapter three, which treats of crimes arising within the maritime and territorial jurisdiction of the United States. It provides that "every person who commits murder, . . . within any fort, arsenal, dock-yard, magazine, or in any other place or district of country under the exclusive jurisdiction of the United States, . . . shall suffer death. "Title XXVIII. of the Revised Statutes relates to Indians, and the sub-title of chapter four is, Government of Indian Country. It embraces many provisions regulating the subject of intercourse and trade with the Indians in the Indian country, and imposes penalties and punishments for various violations of them. Section 2142 provides for the punishment of assaults with deadly weapons and intent, by Indians upon white persons, and by white persons upon Indians. . .

SEC. 2145. Except as to crimes, the punishment of which is expressly provided for in this title, the general laws of the United States as to the punishment of crimes committed in any place within the sole and exclusive jurisdiction of the United States. . . shall extend to the Indian country.

SEC. 2146. The preceding section shall not be construed to extend to [crimes committed by one Indian against the person or property of another Indian, nor to] any Indian committing any offence in the Indian country who has been punished by the local law of the tribe, or to any case where by treaty stipulations the exclusive jurisdiction over such offences is or may be secured to the Indian tribes respectively."

. . . .The first section of the Indian Intercourse Act of June 30th, 1834, 4 Stat. 729, defines the Indian country as follows: That all that part of the United States west of the Mississippi, and not within the States of Missouri and Louisiana, or the Territory of Arkansas, and, also, that part of the United States east of the Mississippi River, and not within any State to which the Indian title has not been extinguished, for the purposes of this act, be taken and be deemed to be the Indian country."

[T]he first article of the treaty of 1868, [states] that "if bad men among the Indians shall commit a wrong or depredation upon the person or property of any one, white, black, or Indian, subject to the authority of the United States and at peace therewith, the Indians herein named solemnly agree that they will, upon proof made to their agent and notice by him, deliver up the wrong-doer to the United States, to be tried and punished according to its laws."

But it is quite clear from the context that this does not cover the present case of an alleged wrong committed by one Indian upon the person of another of the same tribe. The provision must be construed with its counterpart, just preceding it, which provides for the punishment by the United States of any bad men among the whites, or among other people subject to their authority, who shall commit any wrong upon the person or property of the Indians. Here are two parties, among whom, respectively, there may be individuals guilty of a wrong against one of the other -- one is the party of whites and their allies, the other is the tribe of Indians with whom the treaty is made. In each case the guilty party is to be tried and punished by the United States, and in case the offender is one of the Indians who are parties to the treaty, the agreement is that he shall be delivered up. In case of refusal, deduction is to be made from the annuities payable to the tribe, for compensation to the injured person, a provision which points quite distinctly to the conclusion that the injured person cannot himself be one of the same tribe. Similar provisions for the extradition of criminals are to be found in most of the treaties with the Indian tribes, as far back, at least, as that concluded at Hopewell with the Cherokees, November 28th, 1785, 7 Stat. 18. The second of these provisions, that are supposed to justify the jurisdiction asserted in the present case, is the eighth article of the agreement, embodied in the act of 1877, in which it is declared:" And Congress shall, by appropriate legislation, secure to them an orderly government; they shall be subject to the laws of the United States, and each individual shall be protected in his rights of property, person, and life." It is equally clear, in our opinion, that the words can have no such effect as that claimed for them. The pledge to secure to these people, with whom the United States was contracting as a distinct political body, an orderly government, by appropriate legislation thereafter to be framed and enacted, necessarily implies, having regard to all the circumstances attending the transaction, that among the arts of civilized life, which it was the very purpose of all these arrangements to introduce and naturalize among them, was the highest and best of all, that of self-government, the regulation by themselves of their own domestic affairs, the maintenance of order and peace among their own members by the administration of their own laws and customs. They were nevertheless to be subject to the laws of the United States, not in the sense of citizens, but, as they had always been, as wards subject to a guardian; not as individuals, constituted members of the political community of the United States, with a voice in the selection of representatives and the framing of the laws, but as a dependent community who were in a state of pupilage, advancing from the condition of a savage tribe to that of a people who, through the discipline of labor and by education, it was hoped might become a self-supporting and self-governed society. The laws to which they were declared to be subject were the laws then existing, and which applied to them as Indians, and, of course, included the very statute under consideration, which excepted from the operation of the general laws of the United States, otherwise applicable, the very case of the prisoner. Declaring them subject to the laws made them so, if it effected any change in their situation, only in respect to laws in force and existing, and did not effect any change in the laws themselves. The phrase cannot, we think, have any more extensive meaning than an acknowledgment of their allegiance as Indians to the laws of the United States, made or to be made in the exercise of legislative authority over them as such. The corresponding obligation of protection on the part of the government is immediately connected with it, in the declaration that each individual shall be protected in his rights of property, person, and life; and that obligation was to be fulfilled by the enforcement of the laws then existing appropriate to these objects, and by that future appropriate legislation which was promised to secure to them an orderly government. The expressions contained in these clauses must be taken in connection with the entire scheme of the agreement as framed, including those parts not finally adopted, as throwing light on the meaning of the remainder; and looking at the purpose so clearly disclosed in that, of the removal of the whole body of the Sioux nation to the Indian Territory proper, which was not consented to, it is manifest that the provisions had reference to their establishment as a people upon a defined reservation as a permanent home, who were to be urged, as far as it could successfully be done, into the practice of agriculture, and whose children were to be taught the arts and industry of civilized life, and that it was no part of the design to treat the individuals as separately responsible and amenable, in all their personal and domestic relations with each other, to the general laws of the United States, outside of those which were enacted expressly with reference to them as members of an Indian tribe.

. . . offences committed by Indians against white persons and by white persons against Indians were specifically enumerated and defined, and those by Indians against each other were left to be dealt with by each tribe for itself, according to its local customs. The policy of the government in that respect has been uniform. . .

To give to the clauses in the treaty of 1868 and the agreement of 1877 effect, so as to uphold the jurisdiction exercised in this case, would be to reverse in this instance the general policy of the government towards the Indians, as declared in many statutes and treaties, and recognized in many decisions of this court, from the beginning to the present time. To justify such a departure, in such a case, requires a clear expression of the intention of Congress, and that we have not been able to find.

. . . It results that the First District Court of Dakota was without jurisdiction to find or try the indictment against the prisoner, that the conviction and sentence are void, and that his imprisonment is illegal. The writs of habeas corpus and certiorari prayed for will accordingly be issued.

Crow Dog prevailed and was released from confinement and potentially the death penalty, but the case created the political will to pass the Major Crimes Act. The public outcry over this settlement, without the Anglo-American approach to trial and punishment for the crime of murder, led to the passage of the Major Crimes Act, which took self-government away from tribes when any of the major crimes were committed by Indians, even against other Indians.

The Major Crimes Act was passed as a rider to a general appropriations act which extended federal jurisdiction over all Indians for seven major crimes: murder, manslaughter, rape, assault with intent to kill, arson, burglary, and larceny. Questions over criminal jurisdiction continued to be raised in the courtroom over the next one hundred years.

Are Indians U.S. citizens?

In the next case, the U.S. Supreme Court addressed the question, whether an Indian is a citizen?

In the next case, *Elk v. Wilkins*, the U.S. Supreme Court in 1884 held that Indians are not citizens and therefore ineligible to vote, in a narrow reading of the Fifteenth Amendment, which granted the right to vote to all citizens. Justice Harlan had a strong dissent, finding that it was

82

obvious that Indians were given citizenship if they had left their tribal nations.

Elk v. Wilkins
Supreme Court of the United States
112 U.S. 94 (1884)

[This is a petition asking for a review of the opinion from the U.S. District Court of Nebraska]

This is an action brought by an Indian, in the Circuit Court of the United States for the District of Nebraska, against the registrar of one of the wards of the city of Omaha, for refusing to register him as a qualified voter therein. The petition was as follows: "John Elk, plaintiff, complains of Charles Wilkins, defendant, and avers that the matter in dispute herein exceeds the sum of five hundred dollars, to wit, the sum of six thousand dollars, and that the matter in dispute herein arises under the Constitution and laws of the United States; and, for cause of action against the defendant, avers that he, the plaintiff, is an Indian, and was born within the United States; that more than one year prior to the grievances hereinafter complained of he had severed his tribal relation to the Indian tribes, and had fully and completely surrendered himself to the jurisdiction of the United States, and still so continues subject to the jurisdiction of the United States; and avers that, under and by virtue of the Fourteenth Amendment to the Constitution of the United States, he is a citizen of the United States, and entitled to the right and privilege of citizens of the United States. "That on the sixth day of April, 1880, there was held in the city of Omaha, (a city of the first class, incorporated under the general laws of the State of Nebraska providing for the incorporation of cities of the first class,) a general election for the election of members of the city council and other officers for said city. "That the defendant, Charles Wilkins, held the office of and

83

acted as registrar in the fifth ward of said city, and that as said registrar it was the duty of such defendant to register the names of all persons entitled to exercise the elective franchise in said ward of said city at said general election. . . ."That on or about the fifth day of April, 1880, and prior to said election, this plaintiff presented himself to said Charles Wilkins, as such registrar, at his office, for the purpose of having his name registered as a qualified voter, as provided by law, and complied with all the provisions of the statutes in that regard, and claimed that, under the Fourteenth and Fifteenth Amendments to the Constitution of the United States, he was a citizen of the United States, and was entitled to exercise the elective franchise, regardless of his race and color; and that said Wilkins, designedly, corruptly, wilfully and maliciously, did then and there refuse to register this plaintiff, for the sole reason that the plaintiff was an Indian, and therefore not a citizen of the United States, and not, therefore, entitled to vote, and on account of his race and color, and with the wilful, malicious, corrupt and unlawful design to deprive this plaintiff of his right to vote at said election, and of his rights, and all other Indians of their rights, under said Fourteenth and Fifteenth Amendments to the Constitution of the United States, on account of his and their race and color. "That on the sixth day of April this plaintiff presented himself at the place of voting in said ward, and presented a ballot and requested the right to vote, where said Wilkins, who was then acting as one of the judges of said election in said ward, in further carrying out his wilful and malicious designs aforesaid, declared to the plaintiff and to the other election officers that the plaintiff was an Indian and not a citizen and not entitled to vote, and said judges and clerks of election refused to receive the vote of the plaintiff, for that he was not registered as required by law. "Plaintiff avers the fact to be that by reason of said wilful, unlawful, corrupt and malicious refusal of said defendant to register this plaintiff, as provided by law, he was deprived of his right to

vote at said election, to his damage in the sum of $6,000.
"Wherefore plaintiff prays judgment against defendant for
$6,000, his damages, with costs of suit. "The defendant filed a
general demurrer for the following causes: 1st. That the
petition did not state facts sufficient to constitute a cause of
action. 2d. That the court had no jurisdiction of the person of
the defendant. 3d. That the court had no jurisdiction of the
subject of the action. The demurrer was argued before Judge
McCrary and Judge Dundy, and sustained; and the plaintiff
electing to stand by his petition, judgment was rendered for
the defendant, dismissing the petition with costs. The plaintiff
sued out this writ of error.

. . . . The law upon the question before us has been
well stated by Judge Deady in the District Court of the
United States for the District of Oregon. In giving judgment
against the plaintiff in a case resembling the case at bar, he
said: "Being born a member of 'an independent political
community' -- the Chinook -- he was not born subject to the
jurisdiction of the United States -- not born in its allegiance."
And in a later case he said: "But an Indian cannot make
himself a citizen of the United States without the consent and
cooperation of the government. The fact that he has
abandoned his nomadic life or tribal relations, and adopted
the habits and manners of civilized people, may be a good
reason why he should be made a citizen of the United States,
but does not of itself make him one. To be a citizen of the
United States is a political privilege which no one, not born
to, can assume without its consent in some form. The Indians
in Oregon, not being born subject to the jurisdiction of the
United States, were not born citizens thereof, and I am not
aware of any law or treaty by which any of them have been
made so since."

Upon the question whether any action of a State can
confer rights of citizenship on Indians of a tribe still
recognized by the United States as retaining its tribal
existence, we need not, and do not, express an opinion,

85

because the State of Nebraska is not shown to have taken any action affecting the condition of this plaintiff.

The plaintiff, not being a citizen of the United States under the Fourteenth Amendment of the Constitution, has been deprived of no right secured by the Fifteenth Amendment, and cannot maintain this action.

Judgment affirmed.

DISSENT
Justice Harlan and Justice Woods

. . . .Consequently, an averment that the plaintiff is a citizen and bona fide resident of Nebraska implies, in law, that he is subject to taxation, and is taxed, in that State. Further: The plaintiff has become so far incorporated with the mass of the people of Nebraska that, being, as the petition avers, a citizen and resident thereof, he constitutes a part of her militia. He may, being no longer a member of an Indian tribe, sue and be sued in her courts. And he is counted in every apportionment of representation in the legislature; the requirement of her Constitution being, that "the legislature shall apportion the Senators and Representatives according to the number of inhabitants, excluding Indians not taxed and soldiers and officers of the United States army." Const. Neb., art. 3, § 1.
. . . .By the act of April 9, 1866, entitled "An Act to protect all persons in the United States in their civil rights, and furnish means for their vindication" (14 Stat. 27), it is provided that "all persons born in the United States and not subject to any foreign power, excluding Indians not taxed, are hereby declared to be citizens of the United States." This, so far as we are aware, is the first general enactment making persons of the Indian race citizens of the United States. Numerous statutes and treaties previously provided for all the individual members of particular Indian tribes becoming, in certain contingencies, citizens of the United States. But the act of 1866 reached Indians not in tribal relations. Beyond question, by that act, national citizenship was conferred directly upon

86

all persons in this country, of whatever race (excluding only "Indians not taxed"), who were born within the territorial limits of the United States, and were not subject to any foreign power. Surely every one must admit that an Indian, residing in one of the States, and subject to taxation there, became, by force alone of the act of 1866, a citizen of the United States, although he may have been, when born, a member of a tribe. The exclusion of Indians not taxed evinced a purpose to include those subject to taxation in the State of their residence. Language could not express that purpose with more distinctness than does the act of 1866.

. . . .

It was so interpreted by President Johnson, who, in his veto message, said: "By the first section of the bill all persons born in the United States, and not subject to any foreign power, excluding Indians not taxed, are declared to be citizens of the United States. This provision comprehends the Chinese of the Pacific States, Indians subject to taxation, the people called Gypsies, as well as the entire race designated as blacks, persons of color, Negroes, mulattoes, and persons of African blood. Every individual of those races, born in the United States, is, by the bill, made a citizen of the United States."

. . .

Born, therefore, in the territory under the dominion, and within the jurisdictional limits of the United States, plaintiff has acquired, as was his undoubted right, a residence in one of the States, with her consent, and is subject to taxation and to all other burdens imposed by her upon residents of every race. If he did not acquire national citizenship on abandoning his tribe and becoming, by residence in one of the States, subject to the complete jurisdiction of the United States, then the Fourteenth Amendment has wholly failed to accomplish, in respect of the Indian race, what, we think, was intended by it; and there is still in this country a despised and rejected class of persons,

87

with no nationality whatever; who, born in our territory, owing no allegiance to any foreign power, and subject, as residents of the States, to all the burdens of government, are yet not members of any political community nor entitled to any of the rights, privileges, or immunities of citizens of the United States.

Native Americans were not granted the right of United States citizenship until 1924, although they may have been granted state citizenship as part of taking an allotment in the Allotment Act period.

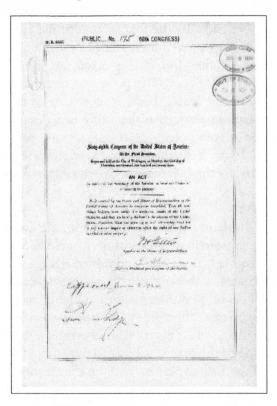

The Act was passed December 1923 and signed by the President June 2, 1924, authorizing the Secretary of the Interior to issue certificates of citizenship to Native Americans. This Act did not distinguish between Indians who had left their tribes and those who remained with their tribes. However, voting law is a state area of regulation and many states continued to refuse to allow Native Americans to vote. New Mexico and Arizona still had laws that prohibited Native Americans from voting as late as 1948.

It was not until 1965 that all states were prohibited by the Civil Rights Act of 1964 from discriminating against voters. Tribes and individual Native Americans in the eastern United States had already lived through the literacy tests that tried to ban all "people of color" from voting. Even if they passed the literacy test they were still often banned from voting.

Final thoughts

The decolonizing of the foundation cases in federal American Indian law approach here provides an overview of general perceptions from viewpoints other than historians who are writing from the documents produced by governments. The stories around these cases and the federal policy periods really do not make sense without understanding the tribal nations and individual Indian perspectives.

Looking further into this retelling of these historic cases that determined the future of Native Americans in the United States, it is important to recognize that each tribal government has their own history, stories, religion and cultural practices that can be told through each of these eras represented by the cases. At the time of each of these cases, many tribes were still not federal recognized and were not subject to the outcome of these cases, but might later be subject to the rules set out in these cases.

Many questions still remain unresolved and treaties are still the law of the land and continue to regulate the relationships between tribal Nations and the United States government.

Made in the USA
Monee, IL
02 January 2022

87713296R00059